PRAISE FOR *RULES OF THUMB*

"This streamlined volume has practically everything our students need in one place."
—Kenneth Wishnia, Suffolk Community College

"Rules of Thumb *is the finest example of a compact handbook/rhetoric that I have ever seen . . . for writers of all skill levels."*
—Suzanne Crawford, Saddleback College

"A handbook with concise writing that is student-friendly. It is an English handbook students actually use."
—Jon Thompson, Kirtland Community College

"This is the only handbook I suggest to writing instructors . . . thorough, yet concise and accessible. Rules of Thumb *skips the gimmicks, skips the inflated teacher talk, and establishes its difference by being a truly student-friendly reference tool."*
—Georgina Hill, Western Michigan University

"Readable, affordable, focused, and a great reference source."
—Melany S. Fedor, Keystone College

"This book fills a need in a way no other text I've seen has, based on its brevity, clear prose, and sensible format . . . I would recommend this book to colleagues who are teaching writing-intensive courses in any discipline."
—Gwendolyn James, Columbia Basin College

"Rules *is by far the most accessible grammar handbook that I've found so far, and this statement is made after many years of teaching freshman composition."*
—Janet K. Stadulis, Lakeland Community College

"Rules of Thumb *is direct, unpretentious, and student-friendly. Its virtues are its brevity and its attempt to reach out to writers in accessible, helpful language."*
—Deborah Mutnick, Long Island University

"It is VERY straightforward —It's to the point and thorough all at once. I am so pleased with this book. I have reviewed and used other texts over the years, and this is the one that more students actually use, read, and glean from."
—Corinna Evett, Santiago Canyon College

By the Same Authors

Good Measures: A Practice Book to Accompany Rules of Thumb

(Exercises keyed to the pages of *Rules of Thumb*)

Rules of Thumb for Business Writers

Rules of Thumb for Research

Shortcuts for the Student Writer

Rules of Thumb for Online Research

(by Diana Roberts Wienbroer)

Writing from the Inner Self

(by Elaine Hughes)

RULES OF THUMB

A GUIDE FOR WRITERS

2009 Update
Includes Latest Guidelines
for MLA and APA
Documentation Styles

RULES OF THUMB

A GUIDE FOR WRITERS

Eighth Edition

JAY SILVERMAN
Nassau Community College

ELAINE HUGHES
late of Nassau Community College

DIANA ROBERTS WIENBROER
Nassau Community College

Published by McGraw-Hill, an imprint of The McGraw-Hill Companies, Inc., 1221 Avenue of the Americas, New York, NY 10020. Copyright © 2010, 2008, 2005, 2002, 1999, 1996, 1993, 1990, by Jay Silverman, Elaine Hughes, and Diana Roberts Wienbroer. All rights reserved. No part of this publication may be reproduced or distributed in any form or by any means, or stored in a database or retrieval system, without the prior written consent of The McGraw-Hill Companies, Inc., including, but not limited to, in any network or other electronic storage or transmission, or broadcast for distance learning.

This book is printed on acid-free paper.

3 4 5 6 7 8 9 0 DOC/DOC 1 5 4 3 2 1

ISBN: 978-0-07-739709-8
MHID: 0-07-739709-6

Vice President, Editor in Chief: *Michael Ryan*
Publisher: *David S. Patterson*
Senior Sponsoring Editor: *Christopher Bennem*
Managing Editor: *Marley Magaziner*
Developmental Editor: *Phillip Butcher*
Executive Marketing Manager: *Pamela Cooper*
Project Manager: *Robin Reed*
Production Service: *Anne Draus, Scratchgravel Publishing Services*
Manuscript Editor: *Frank Hubert*
Cover Designer: *Margarite Reynolds*
Cover Images: *Harnett/Hanzon/Getty Images*
Media Project Manager: *Jennifer Barrick*
Production Supervisor: *Sue Culbertson*
Composition: *11/13 Palatino by Macmillan Publishing Solutions*
Printing: *PMS 307, 45# New Era Matte Plus, RR Donnelley & Sons*

Library of Congress Cataloging-in-Publication Data

Silverman, Jay, 1947–
    Rules of thumb : a guide for writers / Jay Silverman, Elaine Hughes,
Diana Roberts Weinbroer. — 8th ed., [2009 update].
        p. cm.
    Includes bibliographical references and index.
    ISBN 978-0-07-739709-8 (alk. paper)
    1. English language—Rhetoric—Handbooks, manuals, etc. 2. English
language—Grammar—Handbooks, manuals, etc. 3. Report writing—
Handbooks, manuals, etc. I. Hughes, Elaine. II. Wienbroer, Diana Roberts.
III. Title.
    PE1408.S4878 2009b
    808.'042—dc22   2009036805

The Internet addresses listed in the text were accurate at the time of publication. The inclusion of a Web site does not indicate an endorsement by the authors or McGraw-Hill, and McGraw-Hill does not guarantee the accuracy of the information presented at these sites.

www.mhhe.com

To Elaine

Age cannot wither her, nor custom stale
Her infinite variety.

CONTENTS

PART 1: THE BASICS: SPELLING, PUNCTUATION, AND GRAMMAR

PART 2: PUTTING A PAPER TOGETHER

PART 3: THE RESEARCH PAPER

PART 4: STYLE

ACKNOWLEDGMENTS

For their careful reading and questioning of various drafts of *Rules of Thumb,* we wish to thank Beverly Jensen; Polly Marshall, Hinds Community College; Nell Ann Pickett, Hinds Community College; and Larry Richman, Virginia Highlands Community College. Special thanks go to Sue Pohja, of Langenscheidt Publishers, Inc., whose enthusiasm for this book helped to create a trade edition, and to Carla Saint-Paul, University of South Alabama, who offered general support as well as patient advice concerning English as a Second Language. Anne Draus, of Scratchgravel Publishing Services, saw this edition through production with skill, sensitivity, and good humor. Phil Butcher, of McGraw-Hill, has been a friend of our book since the first edition and shepherded us through the details of the eighth edition.

Hannah Silverman made numerous suggestions, both large and small, and Noah Silverman contributed the idea and technical advice for "Shortcuts for 'Word.'" Kirtley Wienbroer helped us with the fine points on a number of pages. In addition we want to thank Ethel and Jimmy Pickens, Peggy Griffin, Ruth Green, and Peggy Sue Dickinson who continue to support our work with their love and spirit.

We are grateful for the encouragement and enthusiasm of our present and former colleagues in the English Department at Nassau Community College. In particular we wish to thank Emily Hegarty, Paula Beck, James Blake, Mimi Quen Cheiken, Kathryn Tripp Feldman, Rosette Finneran, Rebecca Fraser, Jeanne Hunter, Bernice Kliman, Hedda Marcus, Kathy McHale, John Tucker, Dominick Yezzo, and Scott Zaluda; and also Mary Carroll of Lehman College and Leila Sinclaire of Prospect Sierra School. Gabrielle FeBland, a student at La Guardia High School of the Performing Arts, and Michele Guido and Norbert Weatherhead, students at Nassau Community College, also made valuable specific suggestions.

For helping to develop *Good Measures*, we wish to thank Laurie PiSierra, formerly of McGraw-Hill, and Susan Finlayson, of Adirondack Community College. Our thanks also go to John Fitzgibbon, Jane Malmo, and Ernest Migliaccio for their creative ideas. Jennifer Franceschi-Wood graciously gave permission to reprint her research paper.

We also appreciate the thoughtful comments of Kirk Adams, Tarrant County College; Rebecca Adams, Housatonic Community College; Selena Stewart Alexander, Brookhaven College; Jeffrey Andelora, Arizona State University; Andrew J. Auge, Loras College; Janet Auten, American University; Doris Barkin, City College; Judy Bechtel, North Kentucky University; Joyce Bender, Oklahoma Panhandle State University; Michel de Benedictis, Miami Dade Community College; David Bordelon, Ocean County College; Chris Brooks, Wichita State University; Michael Browner, Miami Dade Community College; Timothy R. Bywater, Dixie State College; Joseph T. Calabrese, University of Nevada; Robin Calitri, Merced College; Lawrence Carlson, Orange Coast College; Randolph Cauthen, Bloomburg University; Diana Cox, Amarillo College; Suzanne Crawford, Saddleback College; Natalie S. Daley, Linn-Benton Community College; Ben deSure, Pittsburg Technical Institute; Katherine Restaino Dick, Fairleigh Dickinson University; Ralph G. Dille, University of Southern Colorado; Michael DiRaimo, Manchester Community College; Corinna Evett, Santiago Canyon College; Steffeny Fazzio, Salt Lake Community College; Melany S. Fedor, Keystone College; Susan Finlayson, Adirondack Community College; Nadine Gandia, Miami Dade Community College–InterAmerican Campus; Steve Garcia, Riverside Community College; Ellen Gardiner, University of Mississippi; James F. Gerlach, Northwestern Michigan College; Matthew Goldie, NYCTC; Robert Hach, Miami Dade Community College; Andrew Halford, Paducah Community College; Daniel A. Hannon, Mount Hood Community College; Emily Hegarty, Nassau Community College, Georgina Hill, Western Michigan University; Holly Hill, Everett Community College; Marie Iglesias-Cardinale, Genesee Community College; Gwendolyn James, Columbia Basin College; Goldie Johnson, Winona State University; Richard Klecan, Pima Community College–East; Gina Larson, Kirkwood Community College; Jacqueline Lautin,

Hunter College; Joe Lostracco, Austin Community College; Ellen McCumby, St. Clair County Community College; Mary McFarland, Fresno City College; Jane Mushabac, NYC College of Technology, CUNY; Deborah Mutnick, Long Island University; Kurt Neumann, William Rainey Harper College; Stuart Noel, Georgia Perimeter College; David Norlin, Bethany College; Roger Ochse, Black Hills University; Patricia Harkins Pierre, University of the Virgin Islands; Bonnie Plumber, Eastern Kentucky University; Sims Cheek Poindexter, Central Carolina Community College; Retta Porter, Hinds Community College; Bruce Reeves, Diablo Valley College; Lois Ann Ryan, Manchester Community Technical College; Sara L. Sanders, Coastal Community College; Jim Saxon, Cheyney University; Wilma Shires, Southeastern Oklahoma State University; Patricia Silcox, Florida Keys Community College; Jeanne Smith, Oglala Lakota College; Virginia Whatley Smith, University of Alabama; Janet K. Stadulis, Lakeland Community College; Stephen Straight, Manchester Community College; Jon Thompson, Kirtland Community College; Matthew T. Usner, Harold Washington College; A. Gordon Van Ness III, Longwood College; Kenneth Wishnia, Suffolk Community College; Winnie Wood, Wellesley College; and Mary Zdrojkowski, University of Michigan.

This book would not have existed but for our students—both as the audience we had in mind and as perceptive readers and critics.

Finally, we continue to feel the loss of Beverly Jensen and Elaine Hughes. Beverly, wife of Jay Silverman, helped us in countless ways. Her fine editing eye, clever examples, and ideas for exercises improved each edition, and her encouragement and delicious baked goods sustained our meetings. Elaine, our truly beloved co-author, was at the heart of a collaboration that has always been a joy. A supportive friend, she was also the tough critic who made us pause to reconsider, revise, or even restart. It was this same approach that infused her teaching and her own writing. Above all, she believed in the value of writing—and living—with spirit.

Jay Silverman
Diana Roberts Wienbroer

rule of thumb 1: *a method of procedure or analysis based upon experience and common sense and intended to give generally or approximately correct or effective results . . . 2: a general principle regarded as roughly correct and helpful but not intended to be scientifically accurate . . .*
—Webster's Third New International Dictionary
of the English Language Unabridged. 2002

rule of thumb *A method or procedure derived entirely from practice or experience, without any basis in scientific knowledge; a roughly practical method. Also, a particular stated rule that is based on practice or experience. [First recorded usage 1692]*
—The Oxford English Dictionary, 2nd ed. 1989

rule of thumb *A rough measure or method, without precise mathematical or scientific basis. This term, which probably alluded to using one's thumb as an approximate measuring device, has been around since the seventeenth century. . . . Some individuals have pointed to the "rule" proposed in 1782 by an English judge, Francis Buller, who proclaimed that men had the right to beat their wives provided that the stick used was no thicker than the husband's thumb. Misinterpretation linked it to the cliché, which is about a century older. . . .*
—The Facts on File Dictionary of Clichés, 2nd ed. 2006

This book is for you if you love to write, but it's also for you if you *have* to write. *Rules of Thumb* is a quick guide that you can use easily, on your own, and feel confident in your writing.

We suggest that you read *Rules of Thumb* in small doses, out of order, when you need it. It's not like a novel that keeps you up late into the night. You'll need to read a few lines and then pause to see if you understand. After a few minutes, set the book aside. From time to time, look at the same points again as a reminder.

> Part 1, "The Basics: Spelling, Punctuation, and Grammar," covers the most common mistakes. We put these rules first because they are what most students worry about and will want to have handy. However, when you are writing your ideas, don't get distracted with correctness; afterward, take the time to look up the rules you need.

> Part 2, "Putting a Paper Together," takes you through the stages of writing an essay—from coming up with ideas to proofreading and formatting. In addition, we have included specific instructions for writing an essay in class and for writing about literature.

> Part 3, "The Research Paper," tells you how to conduct a research project with confidence.

> Part 4, "Style," will help you to develop a clear, strong style of writing.

You won't necessarily use these parts in order because the process of writing does not follow a set sequence. Generating ideas, organizing, revising, and correcting all happen at several points along the way.

For further help, ***Good Measures***—containing exercises and writing activities keyed to each chapter of *Rules of Thumb*—is available at <http://www.mhhe.com/rules8e>.

In addition, as a purchaser of *Rules of Thumb,* you have access to Catalyst 2.0, a tool for writing and research at <http://www. mhhe.com/rules8e> where you can go online to find grammar and usage exercises, writing assignments, a source evaluation tutorial, and documentation help.

Rules of Thumb doesn't attempt to cover every little detail of grammar and usage, but it does cover the most common problems we've seen as teachers of writing over the past thirty-five years. We chose the phrase "rules of thumb" because it means a quick guide. The top part of your thumb is roughly an inch long. Sometimes you need a ruler, marked in millimeters, but sometimes you can do fine by measuring with just your thumb. Your thumb takes only a second to use, and it's always with you. We hope you'll find *Rules of Thumb* just as easy and comfortable to use.

Jay Silverman
Diana Roberts Wienbroer

RULES OF THUMB

A GUIDE FOR WRITERS

PART 1

THE BASICS:
SPELLING, PUNCTUATION, AND GRAMMAR

A Word about Correctness

Too much concern about spelling, punctuation, and grammar can inhibit your writing; too little concern can come between you and your readers. Don't let the fear of errors dominate the experience of writing. On the other hand, we would be misleading you if we told you that correctness doesn't matter. Basic errors in writing will distract and turn off even the most determined readers. We encourage you to master the rules presented here as quickly as possible so that you can feel secure about your writing. Once that happens, you'll be free to concentrate on what you want to say.

Commonly Confused Words

A spellchecker won't catch these words. Find the ones that give you trouble and learn those.

---

accept   To take, to receive

Most people do not accept criticism gracefully.

except   Not including

Everybody except the drummer stopped playing.

affect   To change or influence

Affect is usually a verb, so *-ed* can be added for past tense.

Even nonprescription drugs can affect us in significant ways.

effect   The result, the consequence

Effect is usually a noun. Test by seeing whether *an* or *the* can go in front.

Scientists have studied the effects of aspirin on heart disease.

amount   Use *amount* for substances that cannot be counted (an amount of water).

number   Use *number* for items that can be counted (a number of peanuts).

bare   Exposed, to uncover

Is it ever truly possible to bare your soul?

bear   The animal; to give birth, to carry

The surgery allowed her to bear a child.

I do not want to bear the burdens of the entire family.

brake	The mechanism that stops the vehicle; to slow or stop
	Let's put the brakes on these extravagant expenses.
	Brake on the approach; accelerate on the curve.
break	A separation; to shatter or separate into pieces
	After a break for lunch, the ambassadors resumed the negotiations.
	Do not break the seal if you plan to return the software.
choose	Present tense (rhymes with *news*)
	The architect Frank Gehry chooses pliable materials.
chose	Past tense (rhymes with *nose*)
	Napoleon chose officers based on their ability rather than on their family connections.
conscience	The sense of right and wrong
	His conscience was clear.
conscious	Aware
	Flora became conscious of someone else in the room.
desert	Dry country (accent on the first syllable); to abandon (accent on the second syllable)
	After three days in the desert, the lead actor deserted the film shoot.
dessert	Cookies, cake, ice cream, or fruit
etc., and so forth	*Etc.* is the abbreviation of *et cetera* (Latin for "and so forth"). The *c* is at the end, followed by a period. Don't write *and etc.*
	It's better style to use *and so forth*, which is English, rather than *etc.*

fewer, less	Use *fewer* for items that can be counted (fewer headaches).
	Use *less* for substances that cannot be counted (less pain).
good, well	Test by trying your sentence with both. If *well* fits, use it (*doing well, going well*).
	Maybloom is a good shortstop.
	Maybloom is doing well this season.
	Maybloom is doing good when he gives to charity.
	But note these tricky cases:
	Olivia looks good. (She's good looking.)
	Rivka looks well. (She's no longer sick.)
	Clara sees well. (Her eyes work.)
it's	It is. Test by substituting *it is*.
	It's time to find a new solution.
its	Possessive
	Every goat is attached to its own legs.
	No apostrophe. *It is* cannot be substituted.
lay	To put something down
	-ing
	She is laying the cards on the table.
laid	Past tense
	He laid the cards on the table.
	Once you *lay* something down, it *lies* there.
lie	To recline
	As a child, I loved to lie in the hammock.
lay	Past tense (here's the tricky part)
	One day I lay in the hammock for five hours.
	Lied always means "told a lie."

lying	Reclining
	Cleopatra was lying on a silken pillow.
	Staying in place
	The cards were lying on the table.
	Telling a lie
	The manufacturers were lying to the news media.
lead	A metal (rhymes with *red*); to provide direction (rhymes with *reed*)
	Place a lead apron over the patient's body during dental X-rays.
	Gatsby leads a desperate life.
led	Past tense of *lead*
	Ms. Salina led the department for forty years.
like, as	Use *like* to compare two nouns or pronouns (persons, places, things, concepts).
	Larry is not at all like his brother.
	Bonita is a math major, like me.
	Use *as* or *as if* to compare two actions.
	Larry doesn't get easily discouraged—as his brother does.
	It looks as if it will snow.
	Sometimes the verb is omitted:
	Strong as an ox [is].
loose	Not tight (rhymes with *goose*)
	After he lost thirty pounds, his jeans were all loose.
lose	To misplace (rhymes with *chews*)
	My father would constantly lose his car keys.
	To be defeated
	Everyone predicted that Truman would lose.

no, new, now, know, knew	*No* is negative; *new* is not old; *now* is the present moment. *Know* and *knew* refer to knowledge.
on, about, of	Use *view of, philosophy of, feeling about, opinion of* or *about, idea of* or *about*. Do not use *on* in these expressions.
of, have	Remember: *could have, should have, would have*—or *would've*—not *would of*
passed	A course, a car, a football; also *passed away* (died)
	Kirtley passed me on the street; he also passed English.
	Saturday he passed for two touchdowns.
	The coach passed away.
past	Yesterdays (the past; past events); also, *beyond*
	Rousseau could never forget his past romances.
	Proust wrote his novel to recapture the past.
	Go two miles past the railroad tracks.
quiet	Spike Jones rarely played quiet music.
quite	Hippos move quite fast, considering their bulk.
so, very	Avoid using *so* when you mean *very*. Instead of "It was so cold," write "It was very cold," or better yet "It was four degrees below zero." It is correct to use *so* when it is followed by *that:* "It was *so* cold *that* we could stay outside for only a few minutes."
than	Comparison: *better than, rather than, more than, other than*
	I'd rather dance than eat.
then	Time or sequence; next
	She then added a drop of water.
	If you reveal the patient's name, then you face a lawsuit.

the, a, an	• Native speakers of English sometimes mix up *a* and *an*.
	Use *a* before words starting with consonant sounds (*a bat, a coat, a union*).
	Use *an* before words starting with vowels or pronounced as if they did (*an age, an egg, an hour, an M&M*).
	• Students of English as a second language sometimes confuse *the* and *a* or *an*.
	Use *the* rather than *a* or *an* when referring to one specific item.
	I use the small knife for chopping ginger.
	Use *a* or *an* rather than *the* when referring to any one out of a group.
	I use a knife to chop ginger.
their	Something is theirs.
	Wild dogs care for their young communally.
there	A place
	Go over there.
	There is, there are, there was, there were
	There are two main ways to lose weight.
they're	They are
	They're not in a position to negotiate.
to	Direction
	Give it to me. Go to New York.
	A verb form
	To see, to run, to be
	(Note that you barely pronounce *to*.)

too	More than enough
	Too hot, too bad, too late, too much
	Also
	Me, too!
	(Note that you pronounce *too* clearly.)
two	2
wander	To roam aimlessly
	Victoria wandered from shop to shop.
wonder	To question in one's mind
	I wonder what you are thinking.
were	Past tense (rhymes with *her*)
	You were, we were, they were
we're	We are
	We're a nation of immigrants.
where	A place (rhymes with *air*)
	Where were you when the lights went out?
weather	rain, snow, sleet, or hail
whether	If
	No one knows whether he was murdered.
who's	Who is
	Who's there? Who's coming with us?
whose	Possessive
	Whose diamond is this?
woman	One person (singular)
	For the first time, a woman was named as CEO.
women	More than one

All of the women were delighted.

Notice the difference:

This woman is different from all other women.

Remember: *a* wom*a*n; *a* m*a*n

worse	When comparing *two* things, one is *worse* than the other.
worst	When comparing *three or more* things, one is *the worst*. *The* almost always comes before *worst*.
	Exception: The weather changed *for the worse*.
your	Belonging to you. Use only for your car, your house—*not* when you mean *you are*.
	Your relationship with your family changes when you marry.
you're	You are
	You're going to question my logic.

One Word or Two?

If you can put another word between them, you'll know to keep them separate. Otherwise, you'll have to check them one by one.

---

a lot	Always written as two words
	A lot of teachers—a whole lot—find "a lot" too informal.
all ready	We were all ready for Grandpa's wedding.
already	Those crooks have already taken their cut.
all right	Always two words
a long	Childhood seems like a long time.
along	They walked along the Navajo Trail.
a part	I want a part of the American pie.
apart	The twins were rarely apart.
at least	Always two words
each other	Always two words
even though	Always two words
everybody	Jimmy's comments incensed everybody.
	(*Every body* means *every corpse.*)
every day	It rains every day, every single day.
everyday	Fernando put on his everyday clothes.
	(*Every day* is much more common than *everyday*.)
every one	Every one of the beavers survived the flood.
everyone	Everyone likes pizza.
high school	Always two words
in depth	Always two words
in fact	Always two words

intact	Always one word
itself	Always one word
myself	Always one word
nobody	Nobody knows how Mr. Avengail makes his money. (*No body* refers to no corpse.)
no one	Always two words
nowadays	Always one word
nevertheless	Always one word
somehow	Always one word
some time	I need some time alone.
sometimes	Sometimes she slept until 5:00 p.m.
throughout	Always one word
whenever	Always one word
whereas	Always one word
wherever	Always one word

Hyphenated Words

- Hyphens are used in compound words.

  self-employed   seventy-five
  in-laws   happy-go-lucky

- Hyphens make a multiple-word adjective before a noun but not after it.

  George Eliot was a nineteenth-century author.
  George Eliot wrote in the nineteenth century.

  The trip was a once-in-a-lifetime opportunity.
  An opportunity like this comes only once in a lifetime.

  Alfred Hitchcock is a well-known filmmaker.
  Alfred Hitchcock is well known as a filmmaker.

There's no getting around it. Correct spelling takes patience. But you can save time by learning the rules that fit your errors and by using a spellchecker on a computer.

Using a Spellchecker

Always use the spellcheck feature on your computer. However, a spellchecker will miss homonyms like *to* and *too, than* and *then*. It may also give you a different word from the one you wanted. Look for mixups like *defiantly* and *definitely*.

If you use the AutoCorrect feature, be sure to look for automatic changes that you don't want.

Watch Out for IM Spellings

When you IM or text, you often use abbreviated spellings (*u* for *you*). Never use these in a college essay—or even in an email to a teacher.

I before *E*

Use *I* before *E*
Except after *C*
Or when sounded like A
As in *neighbor* and *weigh*.

believe	deceive	freight
friend	receive	vein
piece	conceit	

Exceptions:

weird	foreign	leisure	seize	their

Word Endings

Quiet *-ed* Endings

Three *-ed* endings are not always pronounced clearly, but they need to be written.

used to	supposed to	prejudiced

-sk and -st Endings

When -s is added to words like these, it isn't always clearly pronounced, but it still needs to be there.

asks	consists	psychologists
risks	insists	scientists
desks	suggests	terrorists
tasks	costs	interests

-y Endings

When a verb ends in -y, keep the -y when you add -ing. Change the -y to -i before adding -es or -ed.

crying	cries	cried
studying	studies	studied
trying	tries	tried

When a noun ends in -y, make it plural by changing the -y to -i and adding -es.

activities	families	theories

Exception: Simply add -s to nouns ending in -ey.

attorneys	monkeys	valleys

p or pp? t or tt?

Listen to the *vowel before* the added part.

If the vowel sounds like its own letter name, *use only one consonant:*

writer	writing

The i sounds like the name of the letter i, so you use one t.

If the vowel before the added part has a sound different from its name, *double the consonant:*

written

The i sounds like the i in it, so you double the t.

The same method works for *hoping* and *hopping*. Listen for the different sounds of the letter o.

Here are some other examples:

beginning	dropping	quitting
stopped	occurred	referred

An exception: *coming.*

Words with Prefixes and Suffixes

When you add a prefix or suffix, you usually keep the spelling of the root word.

misspell	suddenness	dissatisfaction
hopeful	disappear	government
unnoticed	environment	

Note: The *-ful* ending has only one *l* (*careful, restful*).

The *-ly* endings also follow this rule—you'll often get *-lly.*

really	totally	lonely
finally	unfortunately	usually

But *truly* does not follow the rule.

Exception: The final *e* is usually dropped before *-ing* and other suffixes that start with vowels.

using	aging	writing
debatable	sensible	lovable

Tricky Words

Look hard at the middle of each word:

de**finite**ly	em**bar**rass	in**ter**est
se**par**ate	ac**com**modate	ne**ces**sary
re**pet**ition	pro**bab**ly	famil**i**ar
o**pin**ion		

CAPITALIZATION

Capitalize the first letter of every sentence and of names of people, localities, days of the week, and months. Do not capitalize for emphasis.

Do Capitalize

- Subjects in school whose names come from names of countries; complete titles of courses

    English   Spanish   History 101

- In titles, the first word and all major words

    The Red and the Black   *Men against the Sea*

Sometimes small words are major: *Death Be Not Proud*

- Family names (*Mother, Aunt, Grandfather*) only when used as a name or with a name (not after *my, his, her, their, our*)

    Papa was cared for by Uncle Manny after my mother left.

- Days of the week

    Wednesday   Saturday

- People's titles when they precede their names

    Dr. Judd   Major Gross   Officer Zublonski

- Brand names

    Kleenex   Coca-Cola   Domino's Pizza

(But not the product itself if it is not part of the company's name—thus, *Crest toothpaste*)

- Public holidays

    Thanksgiving   Fourth of July

- The entire name of a specific place, event, and so forth

    Oak Street   Battle of Gettysburg   Calhoun High School

Do Not Capitalize

- Subjects in school whose names do not come from the names of countries

    history   psychology   marketing

- Genres of literature and art

    novel   poetry   gangster movies   jazz

- Family names (*mother, father, brother, sister, grandfather, grandmother*) except when used as an actual name (*I gave Mother a book*). Do not capitalize *aunt* or *uncle* except with a name (*Uncle Frank*).

    my mother   the grandmother   his aunt

- Seasons of the year

    spring   autumn

- Titles of people separate from their names

    I went to the doctor.
    Two generals and an admiral were consulted.

- Generic names

    facial tissues   soda pop   pizza

- Private celebrations

    birthday   anniversary

- A type of place, event, and so forth

    a dark street   the eve of battle   high school

- Most diseases

    diabetes   tuberculosis   cancer

But note: Alzheimer's disease (the discoverer's name is capitalized) and AIDS

- For emphasis

Do not capitalize whole words (AMNESIA); do not capitalize an entire essay or Internet message.

ABBREVIATIONS AND NUMBERS

Avoid abbreviations, except for words that are always abbreviated.
Spell out numbers that take only a word or two.

■ ABBREVIATIONS

- As a general rule, don't abbreviate—especially don't use
  abbreviations like these in your papers:

dept.	yr.	NY	Eng.	Thurs.	b/c
w/o	co.	&	gov't.	Prof.	thru

- But do abbreviate words that you *always* see abbreviated,
  such as certain titles with proper names and well-known
  organizations:

Mr. Smith	FBI	a.m.
St. Bartholomew	IBM	p.m.

- Abbreviate *doctor* only before a name:

the doctor	Dr. Salk

■ NUMBERS

Spell Out

- Numbers that take only one or two words

nine	twenty-seven	two billion

- Numbers that begin a sentence

  One hundred four years ago the ship sank.
  The ship sank 104 years ago.

- Numbers that form a compound word

  a two-year-old baby

- Fractions

  one-half

- Times using *o'clock, half past,* and *quarter*

  two o'clock   half past four

Use Numerals for

- Numbers that require three or more words

  1,889   162

- Dates, page references, room numbers, statistics, addresses, percentages, and dollars and cents

  May 6, 1974   7,500 residents   99.44%
  page 2   221B Baker Street $5.98

- A list or series of numbers

  1, 4, 9, 16, 25
  seats 12, 14, and 16

- Exact times

  2:00 p.m.   my 8:30 class

- Numbers in papers on scientific or technical subjects

Apostrophes

Most of the time, when you add an *s* to a word, you don't need an apostrophe. Use apostrophes for contractions and possessives.

Do Not Add an Apostrophe; Just Add *-s* or *-es*

To make a plural

two bosses	three dogs	five families
the 1980s	six CDs	Greek gods

To a present-tense verb

He sees	She says	Carol wants

Look hard at *sees* and *says:* no apostrophe.

Add an Apostrophe

To a contraction (put the apostrophe where the missing letter was)

doesn't = does not	it's = it is	that's
don't	I'm	they're
didn't	you're	what's

To a possessive

my mother's car	Baldwin's style	a night's sleep
Gus's hair	children's toys	a family's history
Ms. Jones's opinion	women's room	today's world

To the plural of a single letter or of a word as a word (but not a number)

No *if*'s, *and*'s, or *but*'s	His *g*'s look like 8s.

- If the word is plural and already ends with *s,* just add an apostrophe after the *s.*

  my friends' apartment (several friends)
  my grandparents' dishes

- Pronouns in possessive form have *no* apostrophe.

its	hers	his	ours	theirs	yours

CONSISTENT PRONOUNS

Don't shift from *a person* to *they* to *you* to *I*. Make a conscious choice of your pronouns, especially when you are generalizing.

The problem comes with sentences like

> I got mad; it does make you feel upset when people don't listen.

> A young person has to manage their time well if they want to get ahead.

> Unless someone loves bluegrass music, they won't like this CD.

A person and *someone* are singular; *they* and *their* are plural. Mixing these words in one sentence leads to awkward writing and creates errors. Nowadays you will hear this usage in conversation and will even see it in print, but it is still not acceptable in most writing.

Study the following options:

people . . . they	Instead of *a person* or *someone,* try *people* (which fits with *they*).
	When people know what they want, they can be firm.
a real person	Better yet, use a true-to-life example, a real person.
	My cousin Marc is very firm because he knows what he wants.
	A real example not only makes the grammar correct, but it is also much more interesting and memorable. *A person* and *someone* are nobodies.
he, he or she	The old-fashioned pronoun choice to accompany *a person* is *he.*

If a person is strong, he stands up for his beliefs, even when his friends disagree.

But this choice presumes that *a person* is male. It should be avoided because it is sexist language. *He or she* is possible, but not if it comes several times in a row; *he or she*, when repeated, becomes clunky and awkward.

If a person is strong, he or she stands up for his or her beliefs, even when his or her friends disagree.

Avoid *he/she* and *s/he*.

one

One means a person—singular. If you use it, you must stick with it.

If one is strong, one stands up for one's beliefs, even when one's friends disagree.

One is appropriate for formal writing. Nevertheless, *one* can sound stuffy. How many times can one say *one* before one makes oneself sound silly?

I

Don't be afraid of *I*. It is very strong in writing about emotions and experience. In these matters being objective is not as good as being truthful. As Thoreau wrote, "I should not talk so much about myself if there were anybody else whom I knew as well." A lot of times when you generalize, you really are writing from experience. If you speak for yourself, often you will get to the nitty-gritty of the subject—what you know to be true.

If I were strong, I would stand up for my beliefs, even when my friends disagree.

You don't, however, need phrases like *I think* or *in my opinion* because the whole paper is, after all, what you choose to say.

you

You is good for giving directions and writing letters. It establishes an intimate tone with your reader.

If you are strong, you stand up for your beliefs, even when your friends disagree.

For essays, however, *you* may seem too informal or too preachy. One alternative is to substitute *we* for *you*. In any case beware of mixing pronouns.

Riding my bicycle is good for your legs.

we

We can be used to mean *people in general*. *We* is often a good substitute for *you*.

If we are strong, we stand up for our beliefs, even when our friends disagree.

Be careful that you mean more than just yourself. Using *I* might be more appropriate.

they

They is often the best solution to the *he/she* problem, but remember that *they* must refer to a plural, such as *many people* or *some people*.

If people are strong, they stand up for their beliefs, even when their friends disagree.

no pronoun

Often you can avoid the problem entirely. Instead of

A young person has to manage his or her time well if he or she wants to get ahead.

write:

A young person has to manage time well to get ahead.

I vs. *Me*, *She* vs. *Her*, *He* vs. *Him*, *Who* vs. *Whom*

I, she, he, we, they, and *who* identify the persons doing the action. *Me, her, him, us, them,* and *whom* identify the persons receiving the action.

Pairs: My Friends and I / My Friends and Me

- With a pair of people, try the sentence without the other person:

  My friends and I saw the movie six times.
  (. . . I saw the movie, *not* Me saw the movie.)

  Carter gave the tickets to my friends and me.
  (Carter gave the tickets to me, *not* to I.)

  The same rule goes for *him, her, he, she.*

  The friar mixed a potion for Romeo and her.
  (He mixed the potion for her, *not* for she.)

  Note: Put yourself last in a list:

  My brothers and I fought constantly.
  (*Not* Me and my brothers fought constantly.)

  Beverly read her story to Noah, Hannah, and me.

  Don't be afraid of *me;* it's often right.

  Between you and me, the jazz pianist should have won the competition.
  (*Not* Between you and I . . .)

- Don't use *myself* when *me* will do.

  I painted the whole apartment myself.
  (Here, *me* cannot be substituted.)

  Sam did the formatting for Toby and me.
  (*Not* . . . for Toby and myself.)

  Never write *themself;* use *themselves.*

Comparisons

- Use *I, he, she, we, they* when comparing with the subject of the sentence—usually the first person in the sentence.

    Phil was more generous to Sarah than I was.
    Zachary is more nervous than she is.

    Sometimes *is* is left off the end:

    Zachary is more nervous than she.

- Use *me, him, her, us, them* when comparing with the receiver, the object of the sentence—usually the person mentioned later in the sentence.

    Phil was more generous to Sarah than to me.

    Note the difference:

    He was nastier to Ramona than I.
    (He was nastier to Ramona than I was.)

    He was nastier to Ramona than me.
    (He was nastier to Ramona than to me.)

Who/Whom

- Use *whom* after prepositions (to whom, of whom, for whom, from whom, with whom).

    To whom should I address my complaint?

- Use *who* for subjects of verbs.

    Who should I say is calling?

    When in doubt, use *who*.

Vague Pronouns

Certain pronouns—*which, it, this, that,* and *who*—must refer to a single word, not to a whole phrase. Keep them near the word they refer to.

Which

Which causes the most trouble of the five. Don't overuse it.

Imprecise: Last week I felt sick *in which* I didn't even get to go to school.

Precise: Last week I felt sick. I didn't even get to go to school.

Precise: Last week I had a cold which kept me from going to school.

In the last example, *which* clearly refers to *cold*.

Use *in which* only when you mean that one thing is inside the other:

The box *in which* I keep my jewelry fell apart.

Note that *which* normally cannot start a sentence unless it asks a question.

It

When you use *it*, make sure the reader knows what *it* is. *It* is often weak at the start of a sentence when *it* refers to nothing.

Imprecise: Eleanore ate a big Chinese dinner and then had a chocolate milk shake for dessert. *It* made her sick.

Precise: Eleanore ate a big Chinese dinner and then had a chocolate milk shake for dessert. The *combination* made her sick.

This

This cannot refer to a whole situation or a group of things, so insert a word after *this* to sum up what *this* refers to.

> *Imprecise:* Mr. Charles chats with his employees on their first day of work, he helps them get started, and he raises their pay after the first month. *This* makes a big difference.

> *Precise:* Mr. Charles chats with his employees on their first day of work, he helps them get started, and he raises their pay after the first month. *This encouragement* makes a big difference.

That

Just like *this, that* cannot refer to a whole situation or a group of things. When *that* seems unclear, replace it with what it stands for.

> *Imprecise:* We are not paid well and receive inadequate benefits, but I don't think we should discuss *that* yet.

The reader might ask, "Discuss *what* yet?"

> *Precise:* We are not paid well and receive inadequate benefits, but I don't think we should discuss *benefits* yet.

Who

Use *who* for people—not *which*.

> The runner *who* finished last got all the publicity.

Recognizing Complete Sentences

At the heart of every sentence—no matter how complicated—is a subject-verb combination.

To recognize a complete sentence, you need to recognize its true subject and verb. Recognizing complete sentences will help you to avoid run-on sentences and sentence fragments.

▓ Simple Sentences

- A sentence always has a *subject* and a *verb:*

  I won.

  Philippe snores.

  This soup is cold.

  I, Philippe, soup are the subjects; *won, snores, is* are the verbs. Notice that the verb enables the subject to *do* or *be* something.

  These very short sentences have only a one-word subject and a one-word verb.

- Usually a word or phrase completes the subject and verb:

  Janeen walks three miles a day.

  Suzanne spent all of her savings.

  It's not very difficult.

  She says absolutely nothing.

  They had headaches for two days.

  Robert is her latest fiancé.

  The "blowtorch murders" were committed by the least likely suspect—the grandmother.

  High above the Kona coast in Hawaii stands one of the world's great coffee plantations.

- Sentences can have more than one subject and more than one verb:

  > Tracy and Pete have a new home. (two subjects)

  > They bought an old house and restored it.
  > (two verbs)

- Sometimes the subject is understood to be "you," the reader; the sentence is usually a command or a direction:

  > Avoid submerging this product in water.

  > Walk two blocks past the traffic light.

- Sometimes a word or phrase introduces the main part of a sentence:

  > However, the bar is closed.

  > For example, chemists write CO_2 instead of *carbon dioxide.*

  > Then we drove a thousand miles.

  > At the end of the game, the umpire and the pitcher got into a fight.

  > In the cabin by the lake, you'll find the paddles and life jackets.

For more information about recognizing subjects and verbs, see "Verb Agreement," pages 54–55.

■ COMPOUND OR COORDINATE SENTENCES

Two complete sentences can be joined to make a *compound,* or *coordinate,* sentence.

- Sometimes the two sentences are joined by a comma plus one of the following connecting words:

  > and   so   or   for

  > but   yet   nor

  > Janeen walks three miles a day, but she still eats junk food.

  > Suzanne spent all of her savings, and now she has to start using her credit cards.

- Sometimes the two sentences are connected by a semicolon.

   Grasshoppers are lazy; they are not very hard to catch.

■ COMPLEX OR SUBORDINATE SENTENCES

Sometimes a sentence has two parts—the main part (a complete short sentence) and a *subordinated* part (a complete short sentence preceded by a *subordinating* word). Subordinating words include

because	although	if	whereas
when	after	since	while

A subordinating word signals the start of half a sentence.

   Suzanne has spent all of her savings because her brother is ill.

   Mona shouts when she talks on the telephone.

   The primary market for sea urchins is Japan although they are harvested in Maine.

Notice in the first sentence that "Suzanne has spent all of her savings" could be a complete sentence. On the other hand, "because her brother is ill" is not complete by itself. In the second sentence, "when she talks on the telephone" is also incomplete. In the third sentence, "although they are harvested in Maine" is incomplete.

The two parts of each sentence are reversible:

   Because her brother is ill, Suzanne has spent all of her savings.

   When she talks on the telephone, Mona shouts.

   Although sea urchins are harvested in Maine, the primary market is Japan.

A *compound-complex sentence* occurs when one or both halves of a compound sentence have subordinated parts.

   Suzanne always seemed to be a skinflint, but she has spent all of her savings because her brother is ill.

PERIOD OR COMMA?
RUN-ON SENTENCES AND
SENTENCE FRAGMENTS

To decide whether to use a period or a comma, look at what comes before and after the punctuation.

Often you reach a pause in your writing, and you wonder, "Do I put a comma or a period?" The length of a sentence has nothing to do with the right choice. You need to look at what comes before and after the punctuation to see whether you have two separate sentences or a single sentence with a fragment attached to it.

■ RECOGNIZING RUN-ON SENTENCES (COMMA SPLICES AND FUSED SENTENCES)

The most common run-on sentence happens when you have two complete sentences, but you have only a comma or no punctuation between them. Run-ons usually occur because the two sentences are closely related. Run-on sentences are sometimes called *comma splices* (two sentences with only a comma between them) or *fused sentences* (two sentences with no punctuation between them).

The two most common spots where run-ons occur are

- When a pronoun begins the second sentence:

    Incorrect: The light floated toward us, it gave an eerie glow.

    Correct: The light floated toward us. It gave an eerie glow.

    Incorrect: Ralph decided to move to Paris, he wanted to be a writer.

    Correct: Ralph decided to move to Paris. He wanted to be a writer.

- When *however* begins the second sentence:

  Incorrect: Mosquitoes in the United States are just an annoyance, however in many countries they are a health hazard.

  Correct: Mosquitoes in the United States are just an annoyance. However, in many countries they are a health hazard.

How to Fix Run-on Sentences

Incorrect: I went to Gorman's Ice Cream Parlor, I ordered a triple hot fudge sundae.

The bear got the cell phone now the reporter can't call in his story.

- The simplest way to fix a run-on sentence is to put a period or semicolon between the two sentences:

  Correct: I went to Gorman's Ice Cream Parlor. I ordered a triple hot fudge sundae.

  The bear got the cell phone. Now the reporter can't call in his story.

(Remember that it is perfectly correct to have two or three short sentences in a row.)

Correct: I went to Gorman's Ice Cream Parlor; I ordered a triple hot fudge sundae.

The bear got the cell phone; now the reporter can't call in his story.

- Here are two other ways to fix run-on sentences:

Put a comma and a conjunction between the two sentences. The conjunctions are *and, but, so, yet, for, or,* and *nor.*

Correct: I went to Gorman's Ice Cream Parlor, and I ordered a triple hot fudge sundae.

The bear got the cell phone, so now the reporter can't call in his story.

Use a subordinating word with one of the sentences:

Correct: I went to Gorman's Ice Cream Parlor, where I ordered a triple hot fudge sundae.

Because the bear got the cell phone, the reporter can't call in his story.

Other run-on sentences just go on and on, strung together with *and* and *but.* These need to be divided into two or more shorter sentences.

■ RECOGNIZING SENTENCE FRAGMENTS

Many sentence fragments may appear to be complete sentences, but they have elements that make them incomplete.

Words That Rarely Begin Sentences

Certain words *almost never* begin sentences:

such as	which	
especially	who	
not	whose	except in a question
like, just like	how	
the same as	what	
the way		

In addition, if you have trouble with sentence fragments, it's best not to start sentences with *and* or *but.*

In most cases put a comma or a dash before these words.

Incorrect: We had to drain the pipes after every vacation. Especially in the winter.

Correct: We had to drain the pipes after every vacation—especially in the winter.

Incorrect: They gave him one lousy dollar. Which was a full day's pay.

Correct: They gave him one lousy dollar, which was a full day's pay.

Incorrect: N. C. Wyeth illustrated many children's books. Such as Jules Verne's *The Mysterious Island.*

Correct: N. C. Wyeth illustrated many children's books, such as Jules Verne's *The Mysterious Island.*

Subordinating Words

Certain words always begin *half* a sentence—either the first half or the second half. These are called *subordinating words:*

when	as	if	because
before	while	unless	although
after	since	whereas	even though

A sentence fragment frequently begins with a subordinating word.

Incorrect: Although Janeen walks three miles a day.

When Archduke Franz Ferdinand was assassinated in Sarajevo.

You can fix these fragments by connecting each fragment to the sentence before or after it.

Correct: Although Janeen walks three miles a day, she still has to watch her diet.

Janeen still has to watch her diet although she walks three miles a day.

When Archduke Franz Ferdinand was assassinated in Sarajevo, the whole world was plunged into war.

The whole world was plunged into war when Archduke Franz Ferdinand was assassinated in Sarajevo.

You can also drop the subordinating word.

Correct: Janeen walks three miles a day.

Archduke Franz Ferdinand was assassinated in Sarajevo.

A subtle point: Watch out for *and*. Putting *and* between a fragment and a sentence doesn't fix the fragment.

Still incorrect:	Although Janeen walks three miles a day and she still watches her diet.
Correct:	Although Janeen walks three miles a day and she still watches her diet, she has not yet reached her goal.

Verbs Ending in -*ing*

Verbs ending in -*ing* cannot serve as the main verb of a sentence:

Incorrect:	The boys ran toward the ocean. Leaping across the hot sand.
	Science fiction has its artists. One being Ursula Le Guin.
	I love walking in the evening and taking in nature's beauty. The sun setting over the prairie. The wind blowing the tall grass.

One solution is to connect the fragment to the preceding sentence.

Correct:	The boys ran toward the ocean, leaping across the hot sand.
	Science fiction has its artists, one being Ursula Le Guin.
	I love walking in the evening and taking in nature's beauty—the sun setting over the prairie and the wind blowing the tall grass.

The second solution is to change the -*ing* verb to a complete verb.

Correct:	The boys ran toward the ocean. They leaped across the hot sand.
	Science fiction has its artists. One is Ursula Le Guin.

An -*ing* verb *can* begin a sentence if a complete verb comes later.

Correct:	Leaping across the hot sand hurts my feet.

To **Verbs**

To verbs *(to be, to feel)* also frequently begin fragments.

> *Incorrect:* I went back home to talk to my father. To tell him how I felt.
>
> Keep the hair dryer away from the sink. To avoid submersion in water.

Fix these fragments by connecting them to the sentence before or by adding a subject and verb:

> *Correct:* I went back home to talk to my father, to tell him how I felt.
>
> I went back home to talk to my father. I needed to tell him how I felt.
>
> Keep the hair dryer away from the sink to avoid submersion in water.
>
> Keep the hair dryer away from the sink. You must avoid submerging it in water.

A *to* verb can begin a sentence if a complete verb comes later.

> *Correct:* To talk to my father always calms me down.

Repeated Words

A repeated word can create a fragment.

> *Incorrect:* Dunsworth is the ideal cat. A cat who both plays and purrs.
>
> I believe that Whitman is our greatest poet. That he single-handedly began modern American poetry.

The best solution here is to replace the period with a comma.

> *Correct:* Dunsworth is the ideal cat, a cat who both plays and purrs.
>
> I believe that Whitman is our greatest poet, that he single-handedly began modern American poetry.

Note: *That* rarely begins a sentence, except when it points, as in "That was the year of the great flood."

Using Fragments for Style

You will notice that professional writers sometimes use sentence fragments for emphasis or style. Be sure you have control over fragments before you experiment. In the right spot a fragment can be strong. Very strong.

USING *BUT, HOWEVER, ALTHOUGH*

These three words are used to reverse the meaning of a sentence, **but** they are punctuated differently.

These three words are used to reverse the meaning of a sentence; **however,** they are punctuated differently.

These three words are used to reverse the meaning of a sentence **although** they are punctuated differently.

For further options in using *however,* see pages 39 and 40. For further options in using *although,* see pages 30, 34–35, and 39.

COMMAS

More errors come from having too many commas than from having too few. Here are five places you need them.

Comma Before

> but   and   so   yet   or   for   nor

When one of these words connects two sentences, put a comma *before* it.

> The lead actor was on crutches, but the show went on.
>
> Gina aimed to win the weight-lifting pageant, and that's exactly what she did.
>
> The house didn't sell at $300,000, so they cut the price.

However, don't automatically stick in a comma just because a sentence is long.

> No one at the paint factory could have guessed that the boss would one day be a famous writer.

Commas in a List or Series

Use commas between parts of a series of three or more.

> In one month the game farm saved the lives of a red fox, a great-horned owl, and a black bear cub.
>
> Greg marched to the end of the diving board, took a big spring, and came down in a belly bust.
>
> In the class sat a bearded man, a police officer, a woman eating a sandwich, and a toy poodle.

(Without the last comma, what happens to the toy poodle?)

Don't use a comma in a pair.

> In one month the game farm saved the lives of a red fox and a great-horned owl.
>
> Mary Ellen's mother handed out hard candies and made us sit while she played Mozart's "Turkish March" on the piano.

Comma after a Lead-in

Use a comma after an introductory part of a sentence. Sometimes the lead-in is just a word or a phrase.

> However, the truth finally came out.
>
> For example, you can learn how to fix a leaky faucet.
>
> After lunch, she gave me a cup of that terrible herb tea.

Sometimes the lead-in is an entire clause that begins with a subordinating word (*when, after, if, because, although*). In this case the comma comes at the turning point of the sentence.

> When James walked through the front door, the whole family was laughing hysterically.
>
> If one of the brain's two hemispheres is damaged early in life, the healthy one often takes on the functions of both.

A Pair of Commas around an Insertion

Surround an insertion or interruption with a *pair* of commas. Both commas are necessary.

> The truth, however, finally came out.
>
> Mary Cassat, an American, lived and painted in Paris.
>
> My cousin, who thinks she is always right, was dead wrong.
>
> Peanuts, on the other hand, contain a beneficial fat.

Places and *dates* are treated as insertions. Note especially that commas surround the year and the state.

> The hospital was in Oshkosh, Wisconsin, near Omro.
>
> I was born on August 15, 1984, at seven in the morning.

Commas with Quotations Marks

Use a comma after *said, replied, wrote,* etc., before a quotation.

> Socrates said, "Know thyself."

A comma, if needed, goes inside quotation marks after a title.

> In "The Raven," by Edgar Allan Poe, the bird gradually takes on more and more meaning for the narrator.

Semicolons

Semicolons can be used instead of periods; they also can separate parts of a complicated list.

- Use a semicolon to connect two related sentences; each half must be a complete sentence.

  Ask for what you want; accept what you get.

  One day she says she's at death's door; the next day she's ready to rock and roll.

  I'll never forget the night of the circus; that's when I met the trapeze artist who changed my life.

  It's not that O'Hara's position is wrong; it's that he misses the key point.

  A semicolon often comes before certain transition words; a comma follows the transition.

however	therefore	otherwise
nevertheless	in other words	instead
for example	on the other hand	meanwhile
besides	furthermore	unfortunately

  Schubert was a great composer; however, Beethoven was greater.

  Online travel planning is now the norm; therefore, travel agents have lost business.

  Semicolons work best when used to emphasize a strong connection between the two sentences.

- Use semicolons instead of commas in a list when some of the parts already have commas.

  The three leaders met at Yalta: Churchill, the British prime minister; Stalin, the Russian premier; and Roosevelt, the American president.

  As a child, what your friends have, you want to have; what they do, you want to do; and where they go, you want to go.

Colons create suspense: they signal that an example, a quotation, or an explanation will follow.

Use a colon after a complete sentence to introduce related details. Before a colon you must have a *complete statement*. Don't use a colon after *are, include, such as,* or *says.*

Colons can introduce

- A list

    First, you need the basic supplies: a tent, a sleeping bag, a cooking kit, and a backpack.

- A quotation

    The author begins with a shocker: "Mother spent her summer sitting naked on a rock."

- An example

    Vegetarians often eat legumes: for example, beans or lentils.

- An emphatic assertion

    This is the bottom line: I refuse to work for less than $10.00 an hour.

- A subtitle

    Rules of Thumb: A Guide for Writers

When you type, leave one space after a colon.

DASHES AND PARENTHESES

Dashes and parentheses separate a word or remark from the rest of the sentence.

■ DASHES

Dashes highlight the part of the sentence they separate, or show an abrupt change of thought in midsentence, or connect a fragment to a sentence.

> Alberta Hunter—still singing at the age of eighty—performed nightly at The Cookery in New York City.

> At night the forest is magical and fascinating—and yet it terrifies me.

> Living the high life—that's what I want.

Dashes are very handy; they can replace a period, comma, colon, or semicolon. However, they are usually informal, so don't use many—or you will seem to have dashed off your paper.

When you type, two hyphens make a dash; there is no space before or after the dash. (Computers now can be set to provide a true "em dash.")

■ PARENTHESES

Parentheses deemphasize the words they separate. Use them to enclose brief explanations or interruptions. They can contain either part of a sentence or a whole sentence.

- If the parentheses do not contain a complete sentence, put any necessary punctuation *after* the second parenthesis.

  > I demanded reasonable working hours (nine to five), and they met my request.

- If the parentheses contain a complete sentence, put the period *inside* the second parenthesis.

  Bergman's last film disappointed the critics. (See the attached reviews.)

- When parentheses enclose a sentence within a sentence, do not capitalize or use a period.

  Mayme drives slowly (she claims her car won't go over forty miles per hour), so she gets tickets for causing traffic jams.

QUOTATION MARKS

Use quotation marks any time you use someone else's exact words. If they are not the exact words, don't surround them with quotation marks.

Quotations in this chapter come from the following selection from Mark Twain's *Adventures of Huckleberry Finn:*

> Sometimes we'd have the whole river all to ourselves for the longest time. Yonder was the banks and the islands, across the water; and maybe a spark—which was a candle in a cabin window—and sometimes on the water you could see a spark or two—on a raft or a scow, you know; and maybe you could hear a fiddle or a song coming over from one of them crafts. It's lovely to live on a raft.

Punctuation before a Quotation

Here are three ways to lead into a quotation:

- For short quotations (a word or a phrase), don't use *Twain says,* and don't put a comma before the quotation. Simply use the writer's phrase as it fits smoothly into your sentence:

  > For a fourteen-year-old country boy to use the word "lovely" is surprising.

- Put a comma before the quotation marks if you use *he says.*

  > Huck says, "It's lovely to live on a raft."

  Put no comma before the quotation marks if you use *he says that.*

  > Huck says that "It's lovely to live on a raft."

- Use a colon (:) before a quotation of a sentence or more. Be sure you have a complete statement before the colon. Don't use *he says.*

  > In one short sentence, Twain pulls together the whole paragraph: "It's lovely to live on a raft."

Punctuation after a Quotation

At the end of a quotation, the period or comma goes *inside* the quotation marks. Do not close the quotation marks until the person's words end. Use one mark of punctuation to end your sentence—never two periods or a comma and a period.

> Twain writes, "you could hear a fiddle or a song coming over from one of them crafts. It's lovely to live on a raft."

Semicolons go outside of closing quotation marks.

> Huck says, "It's lovely to live on a raft"; however, this raft eventually drifts him into trouble.

Question marks and exclamation marks go inside if the person you are writing about is asking or exclaiming. (If *you* are asking or exclaiming, the mark goes outside.)

> "Have you read *Huckleberry Finn*?" she asked.
> Did Twain call Huck's life "lovely"?

When your quotation is more than a few words, let the quotation end your sentence. Otherwise you're liable to get a tangled sentence.

> *Tangled:* Huck says, "It's lovely to live on a raft" illustrates his love of freedom.

> *Correct:* Huck says, "It's lovely to live on a raft." This quotation illustrates his love of freedom.

(See pages 106 and 136 for a discussion of punctuation after quotations in research papers.)

Dialogue

In dialogue, start a new paragraph every time you switch from one speaker to the other.

> "Did you enjoy reading *Huckleberry Finn*?" asked Professor Migliaccio.
> "I guess so," Joylene said, "but the grammar is awful."
> The professor thought a moment. "You know, the book was once banned in Boston because of that. I guess Twain's experiment still has some shock value."
> "Well, it shocked me," said Joylene. "I can't believe an educated man would write that way."

Indenting Long Quotations

Long quotations (40 or more words) do not get quotation marks. Instead, start on a new line and indent the whole left margin of the quotation ten spaces. After the quotation, return to the original margin and continue your paragraph.

Here's how it should look:

> Sometimes we'd have the whole river all to ourselves for the longest time. Yonder was the banks and the islands, across the water; and maybe a spark—which was a candle in a cabin window—and sometimes on the water you could see a spark or two—on a raft or a scow, you know; and maybe you could hear a fiddle or a song coming over from one of them crafts. It's lovely to live on a raft.

Brackets indicate that you have added or changed a word to make the quotation clear.

An ellipsis (three periods separated by spaces) indicates that you have left out words from the original quotation. Use a fourth period to end your sentence.

> Sometimes we'd have that whole river [the Mississippi] all to ourselves for the longest time. . . . It's lovely to live on a raft.

You don't need an ellipsis at the beginning of a quotation, only when omitting words from the middle or end.

Writing about a Word or Phrase

When you discuss a word or phrase, surround it with quotation marks.

> The name "Mark Twain" means "two fathoms deep." Advertisers use "America," while news reporters refer to "the United States."

Do not use quotation marks around slang; either use the word without quotation marks or find a better word.

Quotations or Titles in a Series

In a series of quotations or quoted titles, the comma still goes inside quotation marks.

> A common pattern runs through "Good Country People," "Greenleaf," and "Revelation."

Quotation within a Quotation

For quotations within a quotation, use single quotation marks:

> According to radio announcer Rhingo Lake, "The jockey clearly screamed 'I've been fouled!' as the horse fell to the ground right before the finish line."

Quoting Poetry

For poetry, when quoting two or more lines, indent ten spaces from the left margin and copy the lines of poetry exactly as the poet arranged them.

> We are such stuff
> As dreams are made on; and our little life
> Is rounded with a sleep.

When a line of poetry is too long to fit on a line of your paper, indent the turnover line an additional three spaces, as in the following line from Walt Whitman's *Leaves of Grass*.

> I believe that a leaf of grass is no less than the
> journeywork of the stars.

When quoting a *few* words of poetry that include a line break, use a slash mark to show where the poet's line ends.

> In *The Tempest*, Shakespeare calls us "such stuff / As dreams are made on."

Titles: Italics, Underlines, or Quotation Marks?

Italicize titles of longer works, and use quotation marks for titles of shorter works.

- *Italicize* titles of longer works that are published separately such as books, magazines, plays, newspapers, movies, television programs, and websites.

War and Peace	*Newsweek*
NYTimes.com	*The Wizard of Oz*

  Underlining and italics are equivalent; underline when handwriting.

- Put "quotation marks" around titles of shorter works—such as articles, short stories, poems, songs, and chapters—that are found within larger works.

  "The Star-Spangled Banner"   "The Pit and the Pendulum"

  Remember that a comma or period, if needed, goes inside the quotation marks.

  In "Stopping by Woods on a Snowy Evening," Robert Frost uses an intricate rhyme scheme.

- Do not italicize or quote your own title—unless your title contains someone else's title.

  My Week on a Shrimp Boat

  An Analysis of T. S. Eliot's "The Hollow Men"

  The Vision of War in *The Red Badge of Courage*

- Use a colon to separate a title from a subtitle.

  Benjamin Franklin: An American Life

- Capitalize only the first word and all major words in a title.

SHIFTING VERB TENSES

Sometimes you may find yourself slipping back and forth between present and past verb tenses. Be consistent, especially within each paragraph.

Present Tense for Literature

- Use the present tense for writing about literature, film, and the arts.

    Scarlett rushes into the room and pulls down the draperies.
    Hamlet speaks with irony even about death.

- Use the present tense for a critic's ideas.

    Auerbach compares selections from the *Odyssey* and the Bible.

Past Tense for True Stories

Use the simple past tense to tell your own stories or stories from history.

    On a dare, I jumped off the back of the garage.
    President Truman waved from the caboose.

Troublesome Verbs

Had

Many people use *had* when they don't need it. Use *had* to refer to events that were already finished when your story or example took place—the past before the past that you're describing. To check, try adding *previously* or *already* next to *had*.

    Because Jerome had read the book, he wasn't surprised by the ending of the movie. (He *previously* had read the book.)

    When we got to the concert, the singers we came to hear had finished their last song. (They *already* had finished.)

    If I had known about tsetse flies, I would have been much more cautious. (If I had *already* known . . .)

Would, Will

- Use *would* for something that happened regularly during a period of the past.

    In the early days of automobiles, tires frequently would blow out.

- Use *would* when writing in the past tense and referring to something that at that time was projected for what was then the future.

    The producer promised his niece that she would get the lead in the movie. (Use this form if the decision was later made.)

- Use *will* when referring to what is still in the future.

    The producer promised his niece that she will get the lead in the movie. (Use this form if the decision has not yet been made.)

- Use *would* for hypothetical situations.

    Elaine would have preferred to stay home.

    If Jack had called two minutes sooner, Elaine wouldn't be in Japan right now.

    If Jack were more responsible, he would think ahead.

    (Use *were* with a singular subject after *if* or *as though*.)

Could, Can

- Use *could* to refer to the past and *can* to refer to the present.

Past:	Last week the engineer couldn't run the experiment because the ocean was too rough.
Present:	The engineer cannot run the experiment today because the ocean is too rough.

- Use *could* to show what might happen and doesn't; use *can* to show ability.

    My parents make good money. They *could* buy us anything we want, but they don't.

    My parents make good money. They *can* buy us anything we want.

To Verbs (Infinitives)

To verbs can be used with other verbs in present, past, or future tenses. After *to,* always use the basic form of the verb with no added -*s* or -*ed*.

> Dot loved to swim in the ocean at night.
>
> You needed to agree with Professor Grant's interpretation to get an *A* in her class.
>
> We used to visit my grandparents in Italy every summer.
>
> Government officials are supposed to follow the law.

Tricky -*ed* Endings

Often a word with an -*ed* ending is used like an adjective to describe a noun.

> High school students are often stressed by excessive homework.
>
> They have been married for sixty years.
>
> Edna is prejudiced.
>
> I am concerned that Toni is depressed.
>
> The cook will have breakfast prepared by seven o'clock.
>
> Lance gets involved in every aspect of the job.

In these examples the main verb is not necessarily in the past tense; frequently a word with an -*ed* ending is used with the present or future tense. Notice also that the -*ed* word usually comes after *am, is, are, was, were, be, been,* or *being.*

Watch especially for

compared to	embarrassed	stressed
concerned	involved	surprised
depressed	married	used to
divorced	satisfied	worried

Irregular Verbs

Avoid expressions such as *I seen* and *He has went*. Use *gone, eaten, done, seen, written* after a helping verb.

We went.	We have gone.
I ate.	I have eaten.
He did it.	He has done it.
He saw the light.	He has seen the light.
She wrote for an hour.	She has written for an hour.

The Most Common Irregular Verbs

Present	*Past*	*Past Participle* (*after* have *or* be *verbs*)
be, is, are	was, were	been
beat	beat	beaten
bring	brought	brought
come	came	come
cost, costs	cost	cost
do, does	did	done
drink	drank	drunk
eat	ate	eaten
fall	fell	fallen
feel	felt	felt
fly, flies	flew	flown
get	got	gotten
go	went	gone
have, has	had	had
know	knew	known
lay (put)	laid	laid
lie (recline)	lay	lain
rise (get up)	rose	risen
run	ran	run
see	saw	seen

Present	Past	Past Participle (*after* have *or* be *verbs*)
shine (sparkle)	shone	shone
speak	spoke	spoken
teach	taught	taught
think	thought	thought
throw	threw	thrown
write	wrote	written

Verb Agreement

The word before the verb is not always its subject. Look for *who* or *what* is doing the action.

- Two singular subjects joined by *and* (for example, the bird and the bee) make a plural and need a plural verb.

  The bird and the bee make music together.
  My great aunt and my grandfather argue incessantly.

- Sometimes an insertion separates the subject and verb.

  The drummer, not the other musicians, sets the rhythm.
  Two causes for the collapse of their business were employee apathy and management dishonesty.

- Sometimes an *of* phrase separates the subject and verb; read the sentence without the *of* phrase.

  One of the guests was a sleepwalker.
  Each of us owns a Wurlitzer jukebox.
  The use of legal drugs has escalated.

- The subject of the sentence follows *there was, there were, there is, there are.*

  There was one reason for the cover-up.
  There were three reasons for the cover-up.

- Words with *one* and *body* are singular.

  Everyone except for the twins was laughing.
  Somebody always overheats the copying machine.

- Sometimes a group can be singular.

  My family does not eat crowder peas.
  In some states the jury elects the spokesperson.
  A thousand dollars is a lot of money to carry around.

- When *or* or *nor* joins two subjects, the subject that is nearer to the verb agrees with it.

  The attorney or her legal assistants are responsible for the documents.

  Neither the actors nor the director was satisfied with the scene.

- *-ing* phrases are usually singular.

  Dating two people is tricky.

Word Endings: -S and -ED

If word endings give you problems, train yourself to check every noun to see if it needs -s and every verb to see if it needs -s or -ed.

Add -s

- To form a plural (more than one)

  many scientists   two potatoes   several families

- To the present tense of a verb that follows *he, she, it,* or a singular noun

  The system costs too much.   It appears every spring.
  She says what she thinks.   The dog sees the fire
                                  hydrant.
  Bill asks provocative questions. Polly insists on her rights.

  Note: Usually when there is an *s* on the noun, there is no *s* on the verb, and vice versa.

  Pots rattle.   A pot rattles.
  The candles burn swiftly.   The candle burns swiftly.

- To form a possessive (with an apostrophe)

  John's mother   today's society
  Sally's house   women's clothing

Do Not Add -s to a Verb

- If the subject of the sentence is plural

  Tulips come from Holland.
  Salt and sugar look the same.

- If one of these helping verbs comes before the main verb

  does   may   will   shall   can
  must   might   would   should   could

  Kenneth should clean out the back seat of his car.
  Angelica can get there in thirty minutes.
  The professor's attitude does make me angry.

Add *-ed*

- To form most simple past tenses

    She walked.   He tripped.   Mae asked a question.

- After *has, have, had*

    He has walked.   We have moved.   She had already
    arrived.

- After the *be* verbs *(are, were, is, was, am, be, been, being)*

    They are prejudiced against immigrants.
    She was depressed.
    Marge is engaged to be married.

    Note that the *-ed* ending can sometimes appear in present and future tenses:

    The documents are supposed to be ready by now.
    He will be prepared.

Do Not Add *-ed*

- After *to*

    He loved to walk in the early morning.

- After *would, should, could*

    Sometimes she would work all night.
    Charles Atlas could lift two hundred pounds.

- After *did, didn't*

    Harpo didn't talk often.

- After *made, let, helped*

    Her lawyer made me believe she was innocent.
    The moderator didn't let Rob finish his answer.
    The Great Santini helped me understand my parents.

- After an irregular past tense

    I bought bread.   She found her keys.
    The cup fell.   The shoes cost only seven dollars.

For more help with word endings, see pages 13–15, 20, and 49–55.

Parallel Structure

The parts of a list (or pair) must be in the same format.

Not parallel: Lord Byron's travels took him to France, Switzerland, Italy, and to Greece.

Here two of the countries have *to* before them and two do not. There are two solutions:

Correct: Lord Byron's travels took him to France, to Switzerland, to Italy, and to Greece.

Correct: Lord Byron's travels took him to France, Switzerland, Italy, and Greece.

Not parallel: To reach the camp, Marty paddled a canoe and then a horse.

Here it sounds as if Marty paddled a horse.

Correct: To reach the camp, Marty paddled a canoe and then rode a horse.

Not parallel: Immigrants come to the United States to work, to study, because of politics, or simply for a change of lifestyle.

Here the first two parts of the list are *to* verbs, but the next two are phrases.

Correct: Immigrants come to the United States for work, for study, for political freedom, or simply for a change of lifestyle.

Parallel structure can make your writing forceful: see the examples on page 169.

DANGLING CONSTRUCTIONS

Look at your sentences to make sure the parts go with each other.

- There are two problems. In one, a word (often a pronoun) has been left out so that the introductory phrase doesn't fit with what follows.

Dangler: Dashing wildly across the platform, the train pulled out of the station.

This sounds as if the train dashed across the platform. To correct it, add the missing word or words.

Correct: Dashing wildly across the platform, we saw the train pull out of the station.

Correct: As we dashed wildly across the platform, the train pulled out of the station.

Dangler: At the age of five, my mother took me to school for the first time.

Technically, this sentence says that the mother was five.

Correct: When I was five, my mother took me to school for the first time.

- The second problem occurs when a phrase or word in a sentence is too far from the part it goes with.

Dangler: A former weight lifter, the reporter interviewed Terrence Harley about the use of steroids.

This sounds as if the reporter is a former weight lifter.

Correct: The reporter interviewed Terrence Harley, a former weight lifter, about the use of steroids.

This error occurs frequently with *only*. Notice the different meanings of the "correct" examples.

Ambiguous: I only go fishing with Sam on Saturdays.

Correct: Only I go fishing with Sam on Saturdays.

Correct: I go fishing with only Sam on Saturdays.

Correct: I go fishing with Sam on Saturdays only.

Mixed Sentence Patterns

Sometimes you start with one way of saying something, but one of the words slides you into a different way of saying it. Read your sentence as a whole to make sure that the end goes with the beginning.

Incorrect: By opening the window lets in fresh air.

Here the writer started to say "By opening the window, I let in fresh air," but the phrase *opening the window* took over.

Correct: By opening the window, I let in fresh air.

Correct: Opening the window lets in fresh air.

Incorrect: In the Republic of Cameroon has more than two hundred local languages.

Correct: The Republic of Cameroon has more than two hundred local languages.

Correct: In the Republic of Cameroon, more than two hundred local languages are spoken.

Incorrect: Depending on the distance people drive each day will determine how often they should replace their brake pads.

Correct: The distance people drive each day will determine how often they should replace their brake pads.

Incorrect: In "London," by William Blake presents a critique of the modern city.

Correct: In "London," William Blake presents a critique of the modern city.

Correct: "London," by William Blake, presents a critique of the modern city.

Note that these problem sentences most often begin with *by* or *in*.

PART 2

PUTTING A PAPER TOGETHER

What to Do When You're Stuck
Addressing Your Audience
Writing with a Thesis
Finding an Organization for Your Essay
Introductions
Paragraphs—Long and Short
Transitions
Incorporating Quotations
Conclusions
How to Make a Paper Longer (and When to Make It Shorter)
How to Work on a Second Draft
Shortcuts for "Word"
Proofreading Tips
Format of College Papers

Special Case: Writing an Essay in Class
Special Case: Writing about Literature

WHAT TO DO WHEN YOU'RE STUCK

Sometimes the ideas don't seem to be there, or you have only two ideas, or your thoughts are disconnected and jumbled. Sometimes it's hard to know where to begin or what shape your writing should take.

Here are some techniques used by professional writers. Try several—some are better for particular kinds of writing. For instance, lists and outlines work when you don't have much time (in an essay exam) or when you have many points to include. Freewriting works well when your topic is subtle, when you want to write with depth.

▧ TECHNIQUES THAT WORK

Breaking the Assignment into Easy Steps

You can take an intimidating assignment one step at a time. Start where you're most comfortable. Often, once you have some ideas written, one will lead to another, and you'll have a whole draft of your paper. Otherwise, by trying several of the following techniques, you may find that your paper is partly written and you have a clear sense of how to finish it.

Freewriting

With this method you find your ideas by writing with no plan, quickly, without stopping. Don't worry about what to say first. Start somewhere in the middle. Just write nonstop for ten to twenty minutes. Ignore grammar, spelling, organization. Follow your thoughts as they come. Above all, don't stop! If you hit a blank place, write your last word over and over—you'll soon have a new idea. After you have freewritten several times, read what you've written and underline the good sentences. These can be the heart of your essay. Freewriting takes time, but it is the easiest way to begin and leads to surprising and creative results.

Lists and Outlines

With this method, before you write any sentences, you make a list of the points you might use in your essay, including any examples and details that come to mind. Jot them briefly, a word or phrase for each item, in one long list down the page. Keeping these points brief makes them easier to read and rearrange. When you run dry, wait a little—more ideas will come.

Now start grouping the items on the list. If you work on a computer, move related points together; if you are writing by hand, draw lines connecting examples to the points they illustrate. Then make a new list with the related points grouped together. Decide which idea is most important; then cross out ideas or details that do not relate to it. Arrange your points so that each will lead logically to the next. Be sure each section of your essay has examples or facts to strengthen your ideas.

You're ready to compose your paper. You'll see that this system works best when you have a big topic with many details. Although making lists seems complicated, it actually saves time. Once you have your plan, writing the essay will go very fast.

Writing a Short Draft First

On one page, write your ideas for the assignment, what you've thought of including. Take just ten or twenty minutes. Now you have a draft to work with. Expand each point with explanations or examples.

A similar technique is to write just one paragraph—at least six sentences—that tells the main ideas you have in mind. Arrange the sentences in a logical and effective sequence. Then copy each sentence from that core paragraph onto its own page and write a paragraph or two to back up each sentence. Now you have the rough draft of an essay. Remember, your first draft doesn't have to be perfect as long as it's good enough for you to work with.

Using an Audio Recorder

If you have trouble writing as fast as you think, talk your ideas into a recorder. Play them back several times, stopping to write down the best sentences. Another method is to write down four or five sentences before you begin, each starting with the main word of your topic, each different from the others. As you talk, use these sentences to get going when you run dry and to make sure you discuss different aspects of your topic.

Taking a Thirty-Minute Break

Go for a walk, listen to music, meditate, work out—whatever refreshes your mind without dulling it. Forget about your paper for half an hour.

Talking to a Friend

The idea here is for your friend to help you discover and organize *your* ideas—not to tell you his or her ideas. The best person for this technique is not necessarily a good writer but a good listener. Ask your friend just to listen and not say anything for a few minutes. As you talk, you should jot down points you make. Then ask what came across most vividly. As your friend responds, you may find yourself saying more, trying to make a point clearer. Make notes of the new points, but don't let your friend write or dictate words for you. Once you have plenty of notes, you're ready to be alone and to freewrite or outline.

■ TIME WASTERS: WHAT *NOT* TO DO

Don't Start Over Repeatedly

Keep going straight ahead. Write a complete first draft before making major revisions. When an idea comes to you out of sequence, jot it on a separate page.

Don't Use a Dictionary or Thesaurus before the Second Draft

Delay your concern for precise word usage and spelling until you have the whole paper written. Then go back and make improvements.

Don't Spend Hours on an Outline

You will probably revise your outline after the first draft, so don't get bogged down at the beginning. Even with long papers, a topic outline (naming the idea for each paragraph without supporting details) is often an efficient way to organize.

Don't Try to Make Only One Draft

You may think you can save time by writing only one draft, but you can't get everything perfect the first time. Actually, it's faster to write something *approximately* close to the points you want to make and then go back to revise.

Don't Write with Distractions

You can be distracted by music, television, or conversation in the background—or by being too uncomfortable or too comfortable. When you write, you need to focus your physical and mental energy. Choose the space in which you write—it makes a big difference.

Addressing Your Audience

Before you get very far into writing anything, stop and ask yourself, who is going to read this? Considering your audience will guide you in several crucial decisions.

Tone Decide how formal or informal you should be.

- Can you be playful or should you be straightforward and serious?

- Should you include personal experiences?

- Can you use *I*? *I* is usually preferable—it is more direct and more graceful than avoiding *I*—but you do not have to keep saying *I think* or *In my opinion.*

For most audiences, avoid being cute, sarcastic, or slangy; but also avoid being stiff and phony.

Level of Information Think about what your audience already knows about this topic.

- What can you skip or sum up quickly?

- What must you explain?

For example, a research paper about squid will be very different in English 101 than in a marine biology course.

You will need to explain points or terms your audience may not be familiar with, but you must be careful not to fill your paper with tedious information most people already know.

Persuasion Consider your audience's assumptions about the subject and about the position you plan to take.

- What opening will engage their interest?

- What opinions on the subject may this audience already have?

- Which arguments and which evidence will best make your case for this specific audience?

Answer the questions you feel certain your audience will have and find strong counterarguments to support your own position.

The Teacher as Audience

You write best if you write with authority—if you know what you're talking about. But in most college writing the teacher is the authority. Often students feel intimidated and merely try to guess what the teacher wants. Instead, look for issues that are real to you, aspects of the subject that you've considered in the past, aspects of the subject that you respond to strongly. Articulate these ideas and responses, but present them in a way that will share them with your teacher and that builds on what you have learned in class.

In some writing classes your audience also includes your classmates. You can imagine reading your paper aloud to a group of them. Imagining faces as you write can inspire you to say what you most care about.

Writing in Your Profession

For a business or other professional audience, there are additional requirements to consider. Above all, don't waste your reader's time!

- Put the main point up front and highlight the important facts.

- Be very direct and clear, rather than subtly building up to your point.

- Use professional terminology when necessary, but avoid any unnecessary jargon.

- Avoid lengthy examples.

One caution: you don't know who will end up reading a letter or report. On the Internet a document may be forwarded to many thousands of people. Bear in mind the secondary audience—in some cases your writing could even become evidence in a court of law.

When you don't have a clear sense of your audience, imagine people in front of you (make it a large group) and the questions they might ask about your topic. Answer those questions on paper and you will be aiming your essay at a general audience—the audience most essays are written for.

WRITING WITH A THESIS

Your *thesis* is the point of your paper—the point you are demonstrating or proving. It can be stated in a sentence, the *thesis sentence*, that sums up your whole essay and states its purpose. Nearly all college writing sets out to persuade the reader of an idea: that idea is the *thesis* you are presenting.

When You Know Your Thesis

Sometimes you know exactly what you want to show the reader, the point you want to make. In that case you should line up your evidence and your reasoning. What do you need to explain to make your point understandable? What arguments might be used against your point? How would you respond to them?

Be prepared to revise your thesis. As you present evidence, you may discover that your original formulation is not exactly what you mean or that you need to modify it to be more truthful. Go back and build your essay toward your new, more accurate thesis.

When You Don't Know Your Thesis

Often you have a general topic but no point you are trying to prove. Three questions might be helpful:

- What do I find important about this topic?

- What do my examples prove?

- What have I read or heard that I disagree with?

Based on these questions, write a *hypothesis*—a preliminary thesis. Then go ahead and write a draft of your paper. Frequently, you discover what all the details mean only after you've written them out and examined them. In the process of writing, you will clarify just what you want the paper to show and can then rewrite it, cutting out ideas that no longer fit and strengthening the support for your real thesis.

Phrasing Your Thesis

Most college papers state the thesis in a single sentence. (Occasionally, the thesis requires two sentences.) Your thesis sentence should not simply state the general topic or the parts of your paper. You need to take a stand—state a position you intend to prove.

> The seeds of World War II were sown at the end of World War I.

> Misreading the patient's symptoms can lead to disaster, even death.

- Sometimes the thesis can be a simple sentence.

> Jazz is a metaphor for the American experience.

- Often the thesis is a complex sentence that ties together two ideas.

> When shopping malls replaced downtown stores, the economy of inner cities declined.

- The thesis may include a list.

> The cell phone has changed the style and content of communications: in the business world, in families, and even in foreign relations.

As you write your paper, keep improving your thesis statement by narrowing it, making it more specific, more accurate.

Where to State Your Thesis

Feature your thesis where it will have the most impact. In most college essays, state your thesis in a sentence or two near the beginning of the essay—in either the first or second paragraph.

Here are five approaches to positioning your thesis sentence:

- First introduce the general topic or problem and then state your position. (This is the method most often used in college essays.)

- Start right out with a bold statement of your position.

- Begin with a brief anecdote that sets up your thesis.

- Build up to your thesis. Some essays begin with a question, look at different sides of the question, and draw a conclusion (a thesis).

- Tell how you reached your thesis—explaining your original idea, telling how you learned more about the subject, and leading up to your final position.

When the thesis is not at the beginning of your paper, make sure that its phrasing is particularly sharp and clear. Don't bury your thesis!

Finding an Organization for Your Essay

Your goal in organizing is to produce a sequence of paragraphs that leads the reader to a single strong conclusion. But there are many ways to reach this goal. Some people need an outline; others write first and then reorganize when they see a pattern in their writing. Still others begin in the middle or write the parts of their papers out of order.

No method is the "right" one. Some approaches are better for certain topics; some are better for certain people. Do not feel that you have to fit into a set way of working.

Using a Formula as a Plan

Sometimes a teacher gives you a specific format, but most of the time you will need to discover the organization that best enhances the content of your essay. A formula is especially useful for assignments you must do repeatedly or quickly.

Some topics lend themselves to particular arrangements:

Common Patterns of Organization

five-paragraph essay (introduction, three body paragraphs with topic sentence and support, and conclusion)
chronological (the sequence in which events occurred)
narrative (how you learned what you know)
generalization, followed by examples or arguments
process (the steps for how something is done)
comparison (similarities and differences)
classification (types and categories)
problem and solution
cause and effect (or a result and its causes)
a brief case study or story, followed by interpretation of what it shows
dramatic order (building to the strongest point)

The problem with formulas is that they quite often create boring papers. For most topics you will need to discover the best plan by making lists of ideas and reordering them or by writing for a while and then reworking what you've written.

Creating a Rough Outline

Here's a method that works for many writers:

- Make a random list—in *phrases,* not sentences—of everything you want to include. Don't be stingy. Make a long list.

- Now look at your list and decide which are your main points and which points support them.

- Write a sentence stating your major point.

- Decide on the order of your main points.

- Delete ideas and facts that do not fit your major point. Remember, you can't put in everything you know.

- Decide on your paragraphs.

- Now write a quick rough draft.

When to Adjust Your Plan

Sometimes the trick to good organization is *reorganization.* No matter what you thought when you began—even if you had an outline—your topic may well shift and change as you write. Often you will come up with better ideas, and as a result, you may change your emphasis. Therefore, you must be ready to abandon parts or all of your original plan. Some minor points may now become major points. Most writers need to revise their plan *after* they finish a first draft.

Here are the signs that a paper needs to be reorganized:

- Parts of the paper are boring.

- Your real point doesn't show up until the end.

- You have repeated the same idea in several different places.

- The essay seems choppy and hard to follow.

- Your paragraphs are either too short or too long.

In the end make sure that you know the main point you want the reader to get and that every sentence contributes to making that point clear.

Using a Formal Outline

Many writers like to make a detailed outline in a traditional format because once it's worked out, the paper is just about written—for the most part each major section becomes a paragraph, each detail a sentence. Also, some teachers require a formal outline.

Formal outlines use the following numbers and letters for categories and subcategories:

I. _____

    A. _____

        1. _____

           a. _____

             (1) _____

               (a) _____

               (b) _____

             (2) _____

           b. _____

        2. _____

    B. _____

II. _____

    A. _____

    B. _____

Depending on your ideas, you may not need all of these subdivisions, or some parts may need more subdivisions than others. However, you must have at least two items at each level (roman numerals, capital letters, and so forth). You can't, for instance, have an "A" but no "B." If that happens, it means that "A" is actually part of the heading just above it.

INTRODUCTIONS

Introductions should not be boring! Pretend that you are a reader leafing through a magazine: what opening would make you stop and read an article on your topic?

If you get stuck when writing an introduction, try writing it *after* you've written the rest of the first draft. Often you don't find your real main point until you've written several pages. However, in an essay exam or under time pressure, write the introduction first to indicate the map of the paper.

Here are a few common methods for beginning an essay:

Indicate the Parts of Your Essay

In many academic papers and in technical or business reports, the introduction should indicate what is coming. Write a brief paragraph summing up the points you plan to make, one at a time. Then, in the middle of your paper, develop each point into one or more paragraphs.

> Three factors caused the sudden population increase in eighteenth-century Europe. First, the newly settled colonies provided enough wealth to support more people. Second, eighteenth-century wars did not kill as many Europeans as did seventeenth-century wars. Finally, the discovery of the potato provided a cheap food source.

Sometimes you can indicate the parts of your essay more subtly:

> Although *Walden* and *Adventures of Huckleberry Finn* treat similar themes, the two books have very different tones and implications.

Take a Bold Stand

Start out with a strong statement of your position.

> Millard Filmore is the most underrated president in American history.

Start with the Other Side

Tell what you disagree with and who said it. Give the opposing reasons so that you can later prove them wrong. Be very fair—save your counterarguments for later in your essay. For examples of this technique, see the editorial or "opinion" page of your newspaper.

Tell a Brief Story

Give one or two paragraphs to a single typical case and then make your general point. The brief story can catch the reader's interest and make clear the personal implications of the topic you will present.

Use the News Lead

Write one sentence incorporating *who, what, when, where, how,* and sometimes *why.*

> In 1967 Cesar Chavez found a new way to win a living wage for the farmworkers of California: he called for a nationwide boycott of grapes.

Move from the General to the Specific

Begin with the wider context of the topic and then zero in on the case at hand.

> When we think of "strength," we usually picture physical strength—for instance, a weight lifter. But there are subtler forms of strength. Perhaps the rarest is moral strength: the ability to do what is right, even when it is inconvenient, unpopular, or dangerous. My grandfather in Italy was actually a strongman in the circus, but I remember him for his moral strength rather than for his powerful arms.

However, do not start with a dull, extremely broad generality ("In life people tell stories. . ."). Instead, bring your reader more directly to your subject.

Paragraphs—Long and Short

The paragraphs of your essay lead the reader step by step through your ideas. Each paragraph should make one point, and every sentence in it should relate to that one point. Usually the paragraph begins by stating the main idea and then goes on to explain it and make it specific.

Paragraphs should be as long as they need to be to make one point. On occasion one or two strong sentences can be enough. At other times you need nine or ten sentences to explain your idea. However, you want to avoid writing an essay that consists of either one long paragraph or a series of very short ones. Paragraphs give readers a visual landing, a place to pause; so use your eye and vary the lengths of your paragraphs.

▪ Indent the First Line of the Paragraph

In college papers indent the first line of each paragraph half an inch. In business letters or reports, where you single-space between lines, omit the indentation and double-space between the paragraphs to divide them.

▪ Topic Sentence and Support: The Classic Paragraph Pattern

In many college essays and reports, each middle paragraph should demonstrate one point. The most common format for these paragraphs is to state the point and then give the evidence that makes it clear.

Here is the pattern:

Topic Sentence   This sentence states the main idea of the whole paragraph. Usually it comes first or after a brief transition from the previous paragraph. However, a paragraph also can build up to a concluding topic sentence if evidence is presented first.

Support You can back up your topic sentence by using whatever will make it clear to the reader: explanations of terminology, facts, examples, or reasoning that proves your point. With all of these, make clear how your evidence relates to your topic sentence.

A Wrap-up Sentence A final sentence pulls together the whole paragraph. (This sentence should not, however, introduce the topic of the next paragraph. See page 81 on transitions between paragraphs.)

▪ BREAK UP LONG PARAGRAPHS

A paragraph that is a page long usually should be divided. Find a natural point for division, such as

- A new subject or idea
- A turning point in a story
- The start of an example
- A change of location or time

▪ EXPAND SHORT PARAGRAPHS

Too many short paragraphs can make your thought seem fragmented. If you have a string of paragraphs that consist of one or two sentences, you may need to *combine, develop,* or *omit* some of your paragraphs.

Combine

- Join two paragraphs on the same point.
- Include examples in the same paragraph as the point they illustrate.
- Regroup your major ideas and make a new paragraph plan.

Develop

- Give examples or reasons to support your point.
- Cite facts, statistics, or evidence to support your point.

- Relate an incident or event that supports your point.

- Explain any important general terms.

- Quote authorities to back up what you say.

Omit

If you have a short paragraph that cannot be expanded or combined with another, chances are that paragraph should be dropped. Sometimes you have to decide whether you really want to explain a particular point or whether it's not important to your paper.

■ CHECK FOR CONTINUITY

Within a paragraph make sure that your sentences follow a logical sequence. Each one should build on the previous one and lead to the next.

Link your paragraphs together with transitions—taking words or ideas from one paragraph and using them at the beginning of the next one.

■ A TIP

If you keep having trouble with your paragraphs, you can rely on this basic paragraph pattern:

- A main point stated in one sentence

- An explanation of any general words in your main point

- Examples or details that support your point with the reason each example supports your point

- A sentence to sum up

TRANSITIONS

Transitions are bridges in your writing that take the reader from one thought to the next and help to avoid choppiness. You need transitions between paragraphs that show the movement from one idea to the next, and you also need transitions to connect sentences within a paragraph.

First Check the Order of Your Ideas

If you are having trouble with transitions, it may be that your points are out of order. Make a list of your ideas and juggle the order so that one point leads logically to the next.

Use Transition Words

Keep your transitions brief and inconspicuous. Here are some choices of transition words you can use to underscore certain points or relationships:

Adding a point:	furthermore, besides, finally, in addition to
Emphasis:	above all, indeed, in fact, in other words, most important
Time:	then, afterward, eventually, next, immediately, meanwhile, previously, already, often, since then, now, later, usually
Space:	next to, across from, above, below, nearby, inside, beyond, between, surrounding
Cause and effect:	consequently, as a result, therefore, thus
Examples:	for example, for instance
Progression:	first, second, third, furthermore
Contrast:	but, however, in contrast, instead, nevertheless, on the other hand, though, still, unfortunately
Similarity:	like, also, likewise, similarly, as, then too
Concession:	although, yet, of course, after all, granted, while it is true
Conclusions:	therefore, to sum up, in brief, in general, in short, for these reasons, in retrospect, in conclusion, finally

Use Repetition of Key Words

- Repeat the word itself or variations of it.

  I can never forget the *year* of the flood. That was the *year* I grew up.

  Everyone agreed that Adlai Stevenson was *intelligent.* His *intelligence,* however, did not always endear him to the voters.

- Use pronouns.

  People who have hypoglycemia usually need to be on a special diet. *They* should, at the very least, avoid eating sugar.

- Use synonyms—different words with the same meaning.

  When you repot plants, be certain to use a high grade of potting *soil.* Plants need good rich *dirt* in order to thrive.

  Even though the woman was *handcuffed,* she kept running around, waving her *manacled* hands in the air.

Use Transitional Sentences to Link Paragraphs

Usually the transition between paragraphs comes in the first sentence of the new paragraph.

  Even though Hortense followed all of these useful suggestions, she still ran into an unforeseen problem.

  Because of these results, the researchers decided to try a new experiment.

Notice that, in these examples, the first half of the sentence refers to a previous paragraph; the second half points to the paragraph that is beginning.

Do not make a transition at the end of a paragraph. Doing so seems to be changing subjects within a paragraph.

Incorporating Quotations

A good quotation demonstrates the point you are making.

Keep the Quotations Secondary to Your Own Ideas and Words

Each quotation should illustrate a definite point you want to make. Before and after the quotation, stress your point. Maintain your own writing style throughout the paper.

Don't Use Many Quotations

Too many quotations chop up your paper and lead the reader away from your points. Most of the time, tell in your own style what you have read. Instead of quoting you can summarize (give the main points of what you read) or paraphrase (explain a single point in detail in your own words).

Quote Opinions or Key Phrases—Not Facts or Events

It is important to know what to *quote* and what to simply *tell*. In a research paper do not quote information; in a literature paper do not quote what happened. Instead mention these in your own words. Reserve word-for-word quotations for opinions and for key phrases you wish to discuss.

Keep Your Quotations Brief

Short quotations are the easiest and most graceful to use. Avoid using many quotations of over three or four lines. If you want to use a long quotation, omit sections that do not apply and use an ellipsis (. . .) to indicate the part you've left out. A long quotation should be immediately followed—in the same paragraph—by a discussion of the points you are making about the quotation.

Introduce Your Quotations

Direct quotations should usually be preceded by identifying tags. Always make clear who is speaking and the source of the information.

> John Holt, in his essay "How Teachers Make Children Hate Reading," says, "Many children associate books and reading with mistakes."

Incorporating the author's name and any other pertinent information into your text will vary your quotations:

> Educator John Holt offers advice for how to read: "Find something, dive into it, take the good parts, skip the bad parts, get what you can out of it, go on to something else."

Incorporate Each Quotation into a Clear Sentence

Be certain that your quotations make sense both in sentence structure and in content. If you use fragments of quotations, be certain that they are woven into complete sentences.

> John Holt believes that reading should be "an exciting, joyous adventure."

Note that the three examples in this chapter illustrate three ways to lead into and punctuate a quotation.

Here is the source for the quotations in this chapter.

Holt, John. "How Teachers Make Children Hate Reading." *Redbook*. Nov. 1967: 50+. Rpt. in *Responding Voices*. Ed. Jon Ford and Elaine Hughes. New York: McGraw, 1997. 434–47. Print.

CONCLUSIONS

Don't end your paper with preaching or clichés. Consider, out of all that you have written, what is most important. Sometimes you want a quick summation, but other times you should make several points in your conclusion.

To get a memorable last sentence, try writing five sentences. They can express the same basic idea, but they should be worded as differently as possible—one long, one short, one plain, one elegant. If you write five, you'll find the one you want.

Here are several approaches to writing a conclusion:

Return to Your Introduction

Look back at the issues you raised in your introduction, and say what your essay has added to your initial thoughts. Don't repeat your introduction but build on it.

Summarize

Stress your main points, but avoid repeating earlier phrases word for word. For a short essay (two to six pages) a summary is probably not needed. For a longer essay it can be helpful to the reader. Summaries can be boring, so make an effort to give yours some kick.

Suggest a Solution to a Problem

Come up with a solution you think might make a difference, and tell how your findings could affect the future.

Put Your Ideas in a Wider Perspective

What is the importance of what you have said? Move from the specifics of your topic to the deeper concerns it suggests.

Above all, don't just limp out of your paper. Leave your reader with a strong and memorable statement.

How to Make a Paper Longer (and When to Make It Shorter)

Adding words and phrases to your paper makes it at most an inch longer. Adding new points or new examples will make it grow half a page at a time. On the other hand, there are times when cutting a little bit will make your whole paper stronger.

How to Make a Paper Longer

- Add an example or explain your reasons to clarify your point—or even add a new point.

- Mention other views of the subject that differ from yours: either incorporate them (showing the evidence for them) or disprove them (telling why others might accept them and why you reject them).

- Add details (facts, events that happened, things you can see or hear). Details are the life of a paper. Instead of writing, "We got something to drink," write, "We took water from the stream with Stacey's tin cup. The water was so cold it hurt our stomachs."

- Expand your conclusion: Discuss implications and questions that your paper brings to mind.

but

- Don't add empty phrases because they make your writing boring. Don't fake length by using fat margins, big handwriting, or a large typeface.

When to Make a Paper Shorter

- Condense minor points. Sometimes you think a point is necessary, but when you read your paper to a friend, you notice that you both get bored in that section. Or sometimes you get tangled up trying to make a point clear when you can cover it briefly or cut it entirely.

- Watch your *pace* when you tell a series of events. Head toward the main point or event directly. Don't get lost in boring preliminary details.

- Avoid getting sidetracked. The digression may interest you, but it may not add to the real point of the essay.

- Check to see whether you have repeated any point several times. If so, decide on the most effective place to make that point and make it fully in one place.

- Trim out wordiness: replace a dull phrase with a single strong word; cut words that won't be missed. Tightening sentences makes your writing forceful. See "Trimming Wordiness" and "Using Strong Verbs," pages 172–75.

How to Work on a Second Draft

"Only God gets it right the first time."—*Stephen King*

Revision is not just fixing errors. It means taking a fresh look at your paper. You may need to move some parts of it, add the details of a point you have barely mentioned, or completely rewrite a section. Sometimes it's best to put the original paper aside and write a new one. Surprisingly, this can save you time, and the writing will flow much better.

Computers make revision easier, but they can make it seem too easy. It's not enough simply to patch up a first draft by inserting a phrase or sentence in a few spots or by merely spellchecking.

This chapter offers you a number of ways to improve your paper.

Find the Real Main Point of Your Paper

- Your *real* point may not be the point with which you started. Decide what you are really saying; then go back and build your essay around that idea.

- A big danger is trying to cram in everything you've learned. It's tempting to include good ideas or quotations that seem related to your subject but which distract from your main point.

Look at the Order of Your Points

If you see that you've made the same point in two places or if your paper seems choppy, you probably need to reorganize.

- Make a list of your points in the order you wrote them.

- Now play with the order so that each one logically leads to the next.

- Get rid of points that aren't related, or tie them into other points.

- At each step, help your reader to see your logic.

Give the Reader the Picture

Make sure the reader really sees what you mean.

- If you are telling a story, put in the strong details that convey what the experience was like.

- If you are arguing for a position, fully explain your reasons and lay out the evidence.

- If you are expressing an opinion, tell specifically what gave you that idea.

Look for Strong Parts and Weak Parts

- Add to what's strong. When revising, writers tend to focus on the weak spots. Instead, start by looking for the good parts in your paper. Underline or highlight them, and write more about them.

- Fix up what's weak. Look at the parts that are giving you trouble. Do you really need them? Are they in the right place? If you got tangled up trying to say something that you consider important, stop and ask yourself, "What is it I'm trying to say, after all?" Then say it to yourself in plain English and write it down that way.

- No paragraph should just fill a slot from your outline. If it feels dull, cut it entirely or use part of it in another paragraph.

Read Aloud to Yourself or to a Friend

- Read your paper aloud to hear what's strong and what drags.

- When you read your paper to a friend, notice what you *add* as you read—what information or explanations you feel compelled to put in. Jot down these additions and put them into the paper.

- Ask your friend to tell you what came through. All you want is what he or she heard—not whether it's good, not how to change it. Then let your friend ask you questions. However, don't let your friend take over and tell you what to write.

Get Help at the Writing Center or Learning Center

Your college writing center or learning center is staffed by professionals trained to assist you with your writing. Bring your paper, and a tutor will give you constructive advice. You also may be able to get help online.

Add the Final Touches

- Look again at the proportions of your paper. Are some of the paragraphs too short and choppy? Is there one that is overly long?

- Look at your introduction and conclusion. Experiment with the first and last sentences of your paper by writing the idea three or four different ways—with very different wording—then choose the best.

- Write a title that catches the reader's attention and announces your specific subject.

Shortcuts for "Word"

Here are some tips to save time when you are using Microsoft Word, the most commonly used word processing program. Some of these tips also work in other programs.

■ Setting Up the Document

To insert the current date	Insert Menu > Date and Time
To add page numbers	Insert Menu > Page Numbers
To add a header to each page	View Menu > Header and Footer; type your header into the box
To align your header on the right	Highlight text; Ctrl + R
To avoid numbering your first page	File Menu > Page Setup > Layout; click "different header for first page"
To center your title	Highlight text; Ctrl + E
To set the margins for the whole document or for just a selection	File Menu > Page Setup > Margins
To single-space	Highlight text; Ctrl + 1
To double-space	Highlight text; Ctrl + 2
To customize your toolbar	Right-click on a blank section of the toolbar; click "customize"
To set paragraph indentations	Format Menu > Paragraph > Indents and Spacing > Indentations > Left > + 0.5" Special > first line
To set a hanging indent for a works cited or reference page	Format Menu > Paragraph > Indents and Spacing > Special > Hanging By > 0.5"

Using the Ruler (at the top of the page)

The upper marker on the left of the ruler sets the left margin for the first line of each paragraph; the lower marker sets the left margin for the second and any following lines.

To set paragraph indentations	Click and slide the upper marker to the half-inch point, leaving the lower marker at the left margin
To form a hanging indent for a works cited or reference page	Click and slide the lower marker to the half-inch point, leaving the upper marker at the left margin

A mouseclick at any point on the ruler can set a tab (marked with a little *L*).

Using AutoCorrect (set this up before you type)

To automatically correct errors you usually make	Tools Menu > AutoCorrect; check "Replace text as you type"; then modify the list that follows
To insert a specific word or phrase whenever you type its abbreviation	Tools Menu > AutoCorrect; check "Replace text as you type"; then type in the abbreviation and the word to replace it—for example, "Replace *ppx* with *Peloponnesian*"

Warning: Be careful to use a unique abbreviation (such as one with an *x*); asking AutoCorrect to replace "war" with World War II throughout your paper would create a disaster. You may also find it helpful to keep a list of your abbreviations.

Working with Graphics

To wrap text around inserted graphics	Right-click on the graphic; Format picture > Layout
To adjust the size of the text box	Click on the borderlines and drag
To adjust the position of the highlighted image	Drag it, or press Ctrl + one of the arrow keys

■ USING KEYBOARD SHORTCUTS

You probably already use a few keyboard shortcuts—such as Ctrl + S to save or Ctrl + P to print. Check "keys" under the Help menu to find other two- or three-key combinations, such as those for foreign accents.

Maneuvers for the Entire Document

To undo a change	Ctrl + Z	To use the spellchecker	F7
To redo after undoing	Ctrl + Y	To delete one word to the left	Ctrl + Backspace
To go to the last change	Shift + F5	To delete one word to the right	Ctrl + Delete
To search for text or formatting	Ctrl + F		

Highlight the Selection before Using These Shortcuts

(Double-click on the mouse to highlight a word; triple-click to highlight a paragraph.)

To change capitalization	Shift + F3	To add/remove underline	Ctrl + U
To increase font size	Ctrl + Shift + >	To add/remove bold	Ctrl + B
To decrease font size	Ctrl + Shift + <	To add/remove italics	Ctrl + I

Proofreading Tips

The key to proofreading is doing it several times. Careless errors undermine what you have said, so make a practice of proofreading methodically.

Here are some tips to help you spot mistakes:

Make a Break between Writing and Proofreading

Always put a little distance between writing a paper and proofreading it. That way you'll see it fresh and catch errors you might have otherwise overlooked. Set the paper aside for the night—or even for twenty minutes—while you catch your breath. When you write in class, train yourself *not* to write up until the final moment; give yourself an extra ten minutes before the end of class to proofread your paper several times before handing it in.

Search for Trouble

Assume that you have made unconscious errors and really look for them. Slow down your reading considerably, and actually look at every word.

Know Your Own Typical Mistakes

Before you proofread, look over any papers you've already gotten back corrected. Recall the errors you need to watch for. As you're writing *this* paper, take ten minutes to learn from the last one.

Proofread for One Type of Error

If periods and commas are your biggest problem, or if you always leave off apostrophes, or if you always write *your* for *you're*, go through the paper checking for just that one problem. Then go back and proofread for other mistakes.

Proofread Out of Order

Try starting with the last sentence of the paper and reading backwards to the first sentence; or proofread the second half of the paper first (since that's where most of the errors usually are), take a break, and then proofread the first half.

Proofread Aloud

Always try to read your paper aloud at least once. This will slow you down, and you'll *hear* the difference between what you meant to write and what you actually wrote.

Look Up Anything You're Not Sure Of

Use this book and a dictionary. You'll learn nothing by guessing, but you'll learn something forever if you take the time to look it up.

With a Computer, Proofread on Both Screen and Page

Scroll through and make corrections on the screen. Double-check places where you have inserted or deleted material. Use the spellchecker, but remember that it will not catch commonly confused words like *to* and *too* or *your* and *you're*.

Proofread Your Final Copy Several Times

It does no good to proofread a draft of your paper and then forget to proofread the final copy. Remember: A typo or a printer error is just as much an error as any other error.

Format of College Papers

The following guidelines are appropriate for most college papers. Ask your teacher for any specific requirements.

■ Typing Your Paper

Typeface

- Use a 12-point typeface on the computer.

- Do not use all capital letters, all italics, all boldface, or strange fonts.

Spacing

- Set your computer to double-space between lines; you should get approximately twenty-seven lines per page. (Double-space throughout, even for long quotations.)

- Use a one-inch margin on all four sides.

- Indicate the beginning of each paragraph by indenting the first line half an inch. Do not skip lines between paragraphs.

- Do not justify (line up the margin) on the right unless asked to do so. Justifying on the right distorts the spacing between letters and words, making your paper harder to read.

- At the bottom of the page, use a full last line, unless you're ending a paragraph. It's all right to end a page in mid-sentence.

Spacing after Punctuation

- Leave one space after most punctuation marks.

periods	commas	colons
semicolons	question marks	exclamation marks

- Make a dash by using two hyphens—with no space before or after.

- Make an ellipsis (. . .) by using three periods with a space before and after each period.

- Never begin a line with a period or a comma.

- Never put a space before a punctuation mark (except for an ellipsis or an opening parenthesis).

Emphasizing a Word

Use italics—not boldface or capitals—when you want to stress a word. Better yet, if possible, structure the sentence to give the word prominence.

Dividing Words When Writing by Hand

- Avoid, as much as possible, dividing a word from one line to the next. If you can, fit it on one line or the other.

- If you must divide a very long word, divide only between syllables. To find the syllables, look up the word in a dictionary. It will be printed with dots between the syllables: *ex • per • i • men • ta • tion.*

- Never divide a one-syllable word, like *brought.* Never divide a word after only one letter.

Header with Page Number

Create a header aligned on the right with your last name and the page number on each page. (See page 90 if you don't know how.)

ASSEMBLING YOUR PAPER

Cover Sheet or First Page

Include

- The title, without quotation marks or underlining

- Your name

- The teacher's name

- The course title and number

- The date

If you use a cover sheet, center the title in the middle of the page, and put the other information in the lower right-hand corner.

However, MLA format does not use a cover sheet. With your document set at double space, begin at the first line on the left: enter your name, teacher, course, and date—each on a separate line. On the next line, center your title. Return to left alignment on the next line, and indent the first word of the first paragraph.

Binding

- Staple once or clip in the upper left corner.

- Do not put your paper in a binder or folder unless you have been asked to.

■ SUBMITTING PAPERS ELECTRONICALLY

When you submit a paper electronically, simply attach your document to an email as a *Word* or *PDF* file. Include your full name and the course in the subject heading of the email.

When you post a paper on a website, follow that website's instructions.

■ A WORD ABOUT PROOFREADING

- A typo or printer error counts as an error; it's no excuse to say, "Oh, that's just a typo" or "My printer did it."

- Proofread your paper both on the monitor and on the hard copy. Spellcheck but remember that the spellchecker will miss errors like *to* for *too.*

- If necessary, make last-minute corrections with a pen: Draw a line through the word you wish to change and write the correction above the line.

SPECIAL CASE: WRITING AN ESSAY IN CLASS

A wave of panic—that's what most people feel when they are handed an assignment to be written in class. Some students, feeling the pressure, plunge in and write the first thoughts that come to mind. But your first thoughts aren't necessarily your best thoughts. There's a smarter way to write in a limited time.

Take Your Time at the Beginning

- Reread the instructions carefully. Be sure you're writing what you've been asked for.

- Jot down brief notes for a few minutes. Don't write whole sentences—just a word or phrase for each idea or fact.

- Take a few more minutes to expand your notes. Stay calm.

- Decide on the parts of your essay.

For an Essay about Information, Stress Your Organization

- Write an introduction that indicates the parts of your essay. One simple technique is to give a full sentence in your introduction for each of the main points you plan to make:

   > Sigmund Freud is famous for three important ideas. He popularized the idea that we repress or bottle up our feelings. He explored the idea of the unconscious. Most important, he stressed the idea that our family relationships when we are children determine our adult relationships.

Note how the number "three" in the first sentence helps the reader to see the plan of the whole essay.

- Write a paragraph for each point using the same order as you did in your introduction. In each middle paragraph, restate the point, explain what you mean by any general words, and give facts or examples to prove your point.

- Write a brief conclusion, stressing what's most important or tying together the main points.

This is the pattern for the "five-paragraph essay" which many teachers require for an essay written in class.

For Short Essays on an Exam, Write One Paragraph

Write a one-sentence introduction that uses words from the question and asserts your answer. Then, in the same paragraph, present three facts to support your answer, explaining one fact at a time. Finally, sum up your position in the last sentence of the paragraph.

For a Personal Essay, Stress What You Have Discovered

While the five-paragraph essay can get you by, it can easily become stilted and boring. In a personal essay, you have many more options.

- If you're asked to write about a significant event in your life, begin your essay by describing it *briefly*. Use vivid details to bring it to life. Then use most of your essay to tell what you learned from this event or how it has changed you. Remember to divide your essay into paragraphs.

- If you're asked to give your opinion about a topic, you sometimes can use personal examples to support your position. In your introduction make clear where you stand. Then give each important point its own paragraph with examples. Use your own experiences, your own observations, and incidents you've read about.

- If you can't come up with a strong introduction at first, go ahead and write your essay. In the process you will clarify your central idea; then you can go back to introduce it.

- In your conclusion don't preach and don't fall back on clichés. Say what matters to you or what you have learned.

STRATEGIES TO SAVE TIME

Don't Start Over

- Stick to your plan. If you get a new idea, use an asterisk (*) or an arrow to show where it goes.

- Leave room after each paragraph for ideas you might want to add later. If you are writing in an exam booklet, write on only the front side of the page so that you will have room for insertions.

- If you add or cut a main point, go back and revise your introduction to match the change.

Don't Pad Your Writing

Use a direct, no-nonsense style. Don't try for big words—they just lead to errors when you are under time pressure. Simply state your points and the facts to back them up, one step at a time.

Don't Make a Neat Copy

Copying over wastes precious time, and the copy tends to be full of slips and errors. Instead put a line through an error and correct it above the line; use a caret (^) for a short insertion, and an asterisk (*) or arrow for a long insertion.

Don't Rush at the End

- Stop writing ten minutes before the end of the allotted time.

- Read your essay for content. Don't add to it unless you find a *major* omission. Late additions usually create errors and disorganization.

- Proofread with special attention to the second half of the essay (where rushing leads to errors) and to the very first sentence. Look closely for the errors you usually make. Look for words like *to* and *too, then* and *than.* Check your *periods* to be sure you have no run-on sentences or fragments. Look carefully to make sure that you haven't left out any words or letters.

SPECIAL CASE: WRITING ABOUT LITERATURE

When you are asked to write about literature, make sure of your teacher's expectations. Some teachers want a *summary* of your reading, in which you tell the main points of what you've read, followed by your evaluation. However, most literature teachers want you to stress an important idea about the reading and to demonstrate the details that gave you your idea. Usually you will rely on details from the text itself, but you may also be asked to write a research paper about literature, incorporating information and ideas from scholars in the field.

■ GENERAL GUIDELINES FOR LITERATURE PAPERS

You can adapt the methods described here for writing about other arts such as film, music, painting, dance, and architecture.

Gather Your First Impressions of the Topic

Your first reading should be a time to enjoy the text, to respond without the pressure to come up with answers. A good idea is to keep a reading journal in which you jot down your reactions as they come to you.

After you finish reading the work of literature, write down your first impressions, checking the assigned topic. Write quickly, without pausing, to get your ideas on paper. This freewriting will help you to discover the main idea you want to stress.

Reread the Text

Search for evidence to support your main idea and also for evidence that might lead you to modify it. The evidence could include specific quotations, details, events, or subtleties of style. Make notes as you reread, and mark passages you may wish to quote.

Organize Your Essay

Do not merely follow the order of what you read. Instead decide on your main idea, the points you want to stress, and the best sequence to make them clear.

Omit Plot Summary and the Author's Life

Unless you've been asked to, do not include a detailed plot summary repeating all the events of the story. Remember, the teacher already knows what the book says but does not know your ideas about the assignment. Your job is to show the reader your point about the story, not to retell the story. However, you will refer to details from the plot when you give examples to support your ideas.

Do not include a summary of the author's life in your essay unless you have been asked to do so.

Use Evidence to Back Up Your Points

For each main point, explain which details from the reading gave you that idea. In some cases *briefly* quote the author. After referring to a detail or quoting a passage, always explain why that detail or passage supports your point.

Incorporate Quotations Gracefully

Keep quotations few and, in most cases, brief. Include only quotations that help to show the point you are making. Normally do not quote narrative (what happened), but instead quote opinions, key phrases, or examples of style.

First, make your point. Then lead into the quotation by briefly referring to its context. Make clear whether you are quoting the author or a character. When you quote a character, refer to the character by name rather than to the author.

After the quotation, particularly if it is a sentence or more, comment on its significance—tie it to the point of your paragraph.

For specific skills of quotation, including how to quote poetry, see "Quotation Marks," pages 44–47. For strategies in using quotations, see "Incorporating Quotations," pages 82–83.

■ RESEARCH PAPERS ABOUT LITERATURE

One of the major differences between a literary research paper and other research papers is that in a literary paper your main focus is on the text itself. The research takes second place to your own close reading of the piece you are writing about. In writing a research paper about literature, follow the guidelines for all literature papers, with these additional considerations.

Be Clear about the Assignment

Make sure you understand what you are being asked to do. Are you being asked to compare your ideas to those of critics? Are you being asked to find out about the historical context surrounding a piece of work? The specific assignment will dictate the kind of sources you should choose.

Freewrite before Doing Research

Before reading any critics, freewrite about the topic if your teacher has given you one; otherwise, write about your thoughts and feelings in response to the reading. Write out several ideas that you might emphasize in an essay.

Choose Several Critics to Read

Not all critical studies are equal. To find the best critics to read, a good place to start is with the introduction and any list of recommended readings in the edition of the work you are studying. You can also look at recommended sources in anthologies (such as *The Norton Anthology of English Literature*). The most complete listings of books and articles about literature are in the *MLA* (Modern Language Association) *Bibliography*. Also, your professor may guide you to the best critical studies.

Read the critics carefully and critically. Look for ideas that correspond to your own experience of the work. Be open to reconsidering and refining your first impressions, even changing them completely at times. But remember that your experience as a reader has value and must be the heart of your essay.

Incorporate Ideas of Critics into Your Essay

For most assignments the critics you've read should not dominate your essay. Organize your paper around your ideas, presenting one idea at a time rather than presenting one critic at a time. Don't get bogged down in the ideas of critics. Remember that your ideas are still the center of your paper.

In most cases paraphrase or summarize the ideas of critics, quoting them directly only when their phrasing is significant or memorable—when you will comment on the critic's wording. Always relate a critic's ideas to the main thrust or thesis of your essay.

Remember that your primary subject is the literature itself. It offers the best evidence for your ideas. The majority of your examples and quotations will come from the literary text.

CONVENTIONS OF LITERARY ESSAYS

Titles

- *Italicize* titles of books, periodicals, plays, films, and television programs. (When handwriting, use an underline.) Put "quotation marks" around titles of stories, poems, essays, and one-act plays.

- Capitalize the first word and all major words.

- The title of your paper should express your main idea, not just give the title of the text.

  > The Uses of Rhyme in Robert Browning's "My Last Duchess"

For detailed instructions about titles, see "Titles: Italics, Underlines, or Quotation Marks?" on page 48.

Identifying the Author and Title

- Use the author's full name the first time you mention it. Thereafter, use the last name, never the first name by itself.

- Be sure to identify the title and author early in your essay, even if you've already done so in your title.

  > In "A Fly Buzzed When I Died," Emily Dickinson presents a disturbing vision of the moment of death.

> In *King Lear,* Shakespeare examines a king's assumptions about language.

> "A Rose for Emily," by William Faulkner, is a study of changing social classes.

> Laura Esquivel's *Like Water for Chocolate* explores the consequences of passion.

You can use this type of sentence to begin your essay, or you can introduce the general topic (death, language, social classes, passion) and then identify the specific text you will examine.

Note carefully the punctuation in these examples. Remember that a comma or period goes inside quotation marks.

Using Correct Literary Terms

A *story* is a series of events leading to a climax. In literature courses, "story" refers to fiction. A *novel* is a book-length story.

Essays and *articles* are short works of nonfiction. Essays present reflections and ideas based upon observation, experience, or reading. They may or may not be written for publication. Articles present information and are written for publication.

A *poem* is arranged with *lines* of varying length; some poems are also divided into *stanzas* (groups of lines).

A *play* is a story written to be presented in a theater. It consists mostly of the dialogue of the characters but also contains brief stage directions to describe the set, sound, costumes, and lighting and to indicate actions of the characters.

Verb Tenses

In writing your paper, use the present tense, the most graceful tense for referring to a poem or story.

> Early in the novel, Elizabeth misjudges Darcy.

> Yeats portrays a "glimmering girl" who can never be captured.

Also use present tense in referring to the ideas of most critics. (However, use past tense for critics from before the twentieth century.)

▪ BIBLIOGRAPHICAL INFORMATION

Page References

In your paper indicate the location of each quotation from your primary source by putting the page numbers in parentheses following the quotation.

> The first chapter of Hawthorne's *The Scarlet Letter* puns on the mix of church and state in the "steeple-crowned hats" of the Puritans (35).

If the quotation is indented, put the period before the parenthesis; otherwise put the period last.

- For a poem (such as Coleridge's "The Rime of the Ancient Mariner"), give the line numbers.

  > Water, water, every where,
  > And all the boards did shrink;
  > Water, water, every where,
  > Nor any drop to drink. (119–122)

- For the Bible, give the abbreviated title of the specific book, with chapter and verse.

  > To every thing there is a season, and a time to every purpose under the heaven. (Eccles. 3.1)

- For a play (such as Shakespeare's *Antony and Cleopatra*), give act, scene, and lines.

  > Age cannot wither her, nor custom stale
  > Her infinite variety. (2.2.234–235)

- When quoting or referring to a critic, mention the critic's name.

  > Eudora Welty says that, in *To the Lighthouse*, Virginia Woolf "has shown us the shape of the human spirit" (xii).

Works Cited

Your *Works Cited* should include an entry for every source you cited within the paper, including the edition of the literary text that you have used.

> Hughes, Langston. "Mother to Son." *Selected Poems*
> *of Langston Hughes*. New York: Knopf, 1970.
> 187.

If the book was originally published in an edition different from yours, put the original date of publication after the title:

> Woolf, Virginia. *To the Lighthouse*. 1927. San
> Diego: Harcourt, 1981.

If you used a poem or short story in an anthology or an introduction or a preface from a book, you need to include a citation for the author and specific short work you referred to, as well as all the information for the book, including the pages covered.

> Meltzer, Richard. "The Aesthetics of Rock."
> *Penguin Book of Rock & Roll Writing*. Ed.
> Clinton Heylin. New York: Viking, 1992.
> 81–87.

> Welty, Eudora. Foreword. *To the Lighthouse*. By
> Virginia Woolf. San Diego: Harcourt, 1981.
> vii–xii.

For further details see the chapter "Documentation: The MLA Style," pages 136–49.

PART 3

THE RESEARCH PAPER

SEVEN STEPS TO A RESEARCH PAPER

Here is an overview of the entire research project—from gathering ideas through the final paper. The details are in the chapters that follow.

1. Before you conduct any research, write down what you hope to find out. List specific questions you want to answer. See pages 112–13.

2. Go beyond Google and *Wikipedia*. Find a variety of sources: books, articles from periodicals, websites, and personal contacts. See pages 113–14 and 121–24.

3. Take notes and also get down all necessary bibliographic information. Record page numbers for information you find in books and periodicals. See pages 118–19.

4. Write your first draft without notes or books. Explain your research goals, what you found out (in as much detail as you can recall), and the value of what you learned. See pages 126–27.

5. Use your notes to add facts and brief quotations to your first draft. Choose only the most important. See pages 128–30.

6. Examine your paper to make sure

   • your writing is straightforward (not wordy or artificial)
   • the details will be understandable to your reader
   • you did not go off on tangents
   • the facts and quotations are accurate

   See page 131.

7. Add documentation: a *Works Cited* page at the end and citations (in parentheses) following the facts, ideas, or quotations that came from your sources. See pages 133–35.

How to Conduct Research

Here it comes again, that terrifying request from a teacher for a "research" or "term" paper. You don't have to be scared by the names of these papers. A research or term paper is simply a fairly long paper in which you set forth a point of view and support it with information you've gathered from books, articles, websites, and other sources.

The trouble with many student papers is that they present information one source at a time, pretty much copying from the sources and changing a few words. Instead, a good research paper presents your view of the topic, guiding the reader one idea at a time into what you have come to understand.

■ Write First, Research Second

Your first step is to pinpoint what you're looking for. If you connect right away to the Web or head straight to the library, you're likely to wander around in a maze of information. A few minutes spent defining your goals can save you many hours in the long run.

List Your Research Questions

What do you hope to find out? List all the questions that you want to answer, and mark the ones that have the highest priority.

Narrow Your Questions

Before searching for reading materials, limit what you want to learn; otherwise, you will read yourself into a hole and never get your paper written. For example, if "pizza" is your general topic, you might narrow your questions to

> Is pizza good for you?
>
> How does pizza compare nutritionally with other fast foods?

Notice that these questions avoid committing to one point of view. Another method is to write a tentative thesis statement for your paper, which you will then attempt to prove during your research. You may sometimes have to use two sentences, but try for one.

> Pizza is the most wholesome fast food on the American market today.

In this example the general topic of "pizza" has been narrowed to a focus on the nutritional value of pizza. During research you will discover whether your thesis is true.

■ USE A VARIETY OF SOURCES

Don't limit your research by sticking only to the sources you're most comfortable with. You probably find it easy to search the Internet and difficult to use the library. Or you might know how to find a book in the library but not how to find articles in periodicals. Use your ingenuity to come up with a variety of sources and to track down leads.

Get a General Introduction to the Topic If a topic is new to you, start with a textbook or encyclopedia and then consult any resources that have been cited. You can check *Wikipedia*, but keep in mind that both experts and amateurs write these articles.

Network Tell your family and friends that you're looking for information; ask them to save articles for you and to listen for reports on the radio or television.

Ask an Expert A teacher, businessperson, physician, or other expert on the subject can point you to the most valuable sources. You might even make an appointment to record an interview and get the real lowdown on the topic. If an interview isn't possible, enter an expert's name into a search engine to see whether there is a personal website or blog.

Consult Books, Articles, and Websites In general, books give a more systematic overview of a subject; articles give a more current view of one aspect; websites may do either (or neither). For literary and historical topics, books and some older articles are often superior. However, scientific and technical topics require up-to-date sources, so books may not be appropriate except for background, and in general only the most recent articles and Web sources can be used.

Get a Different Perspective If your subject is not scholarly, try Google Scholar (http://scholar.google.com). For an academic topic, check the archives of the *New York Times* or specialized TV channels—reading about a current production of *Hamlet*, for example, could offer you some good ideas.

Look for Unusual Sources

- Use Google to find organizations devoted to your topic.

- Visit a business, a museum, or another institution.

- Find a documentary video.

- Log on to the website of a relevant government department.

- Read blogs; you can find them with Technorati or Bloglines, where you can also log in with a request for daily updates to your email.

■ USE SEARCH TERMS SKILLFULLY

You'll probably need a variety of search terms to find what you're looking for.

Make a List of Key Words

- Different terms that refer to your subject

- Categories it fits into

- Subtopics

Use Preliminary Reading to Modify Your List

Review class notes, look in a textbook, browse on the Web, or read an encyclopedia article. As you read, modify your list:

- Add specific terms and subtopics.

- Add names of authors and other experts in the field.

As you learn more and more about your subject, keep adjusting your search terms.

Combine Your Terms When Searching

Let's say you're interested in the nutritional value of pizza. You can combine the term *pizza* with terms like *nutrition, health, calories,* and *fat.*

Every search program uses slightly different rules of operation, but most use two searching conventions:

* Quotation marks to indicate that a phrase is to be treated as one search term: "fast food"

This method is a quick way to find an article when you know the exact title or when you have an exact quotation you can't document.

* Boolean operators:

    and specifies that both terms should appear

        pizza and nutrition

    or specifies that either term should appear

        pepperoni or sausage

    not specifies that a term should not appear

        domino's not game

Many search programs provide easy ways to narrow your search. Some invite you to type in a question. However, you will get better results if you submit the phrasing that you hope to find in the answer. For example, instead of entering

    "Can pizza be part of a healthful diet?"

try

    Pizza in a healthful diet

■ CHOOSE THE BEST SOURCES OF INFORMATION

All books and articles are not equal. You will need to reject sources that don't fit your topic. Particularly watch out for:

- Sources that are too old, too specialized, or too superficial
- Sources that aren't relevant to your specific angle on the topic
- Sources that repeat what you already have noted

Consider the level of information you require. A twenty-page paper needs much more detailed information and analysis than a five-page paper. A paper on the nutritional value of fast foods will be much more complex for a class in nutrition than for English 101.

Use both primary and secondary sources. Primary sources are written by those actually involved in the subject; secondary sources are written by people studying the subject. For instance, a speech by Martin Luther King is a primary source; a biography of Martin Luther King is a secondary source. Depending on your topic, you may need to read the original source, not just the interpretations written by others.

Stick to your angle on the topic. As you look through the sources you've gathered, focus on the primary questions you've set out to answer. Don't let a source on a different subtopic lead you away from your goals. You want to be open to new ideas, but one skill of a good researcher is knowing which books, articles, and websites to bypass.

Consult the "List of Valuable Sources" at the back of this book.

Sizing Up a Website

- **What is the address?** Use the Web address as a reminder to check for point of view.

  > **.gov** (government): Is there political bias?
  > **.org** (nonprofit organization): What does the organization promote?
  > **.edu** (educational institution): Is the author a professor or a student?
  > **.com** (business) or **.net** (large network): Is the article selling or reporting? Is this a website for an organization or a private individual?

  In addition, beware of sites that don't list a geographical address.

- **Who are the author and sponsoring organization?** If none is listed, go to the home page or to the base of the address (deleting everything after the suffix, such as *.com*). If you don't recognize the author or organization, check the name in Google.

- **What is the last date of revision?** Unless the information is historical, is the site regularly updated?

- **Are there many typographical or grammatical errors?** (Allow for the fact that English is the dominant language on the Internet, and some authors may be inexperienced users of English.)

- **Do reputable websites link to this one?** Does this website provide links to others of high quality?

- **Does the author provide documentation for the sources of information used in the article?** Do those sources check out when you enter them in a search engine? Look for an objective tone, specific examples, footnotes or references, and careful analysis.

- **Don't let graphics fool you.** A drab website may or may not be trustworthy. Classy graphics may or may not accompany professional reporting.

On page 190, you will find help for checking facts and for identifying false stories on the Internet.

■ TAKE USABLE NOTES

Good notes are brief—you don't want to copy or download large chunks of information. Nor can you write your paper while taking notes. Taking notes and writing your paper must be two separate steps.

Record Bibliographical Information

Make sure you have the details about your source that you will need for your *Works Cited, References,* or *Bibliography.*

For an Article:

- Author
- Title of article
- Title of publication
- Date
- Pages
- Format

For a Book:

- Author
- Title
- City and state of publication
- Publisher
- Date of publication
- Format

For a Website:

- Author (if given)
- Title of page or section
- Name of website
- Date posted or last revised
- Sponsoring organization (if given)
- Web
- Date you viewed it

For Other Sources:

- Author (if known)
- Title
- Details about publication or broadcast
- Date you viewed/ heard it
- Format

Record Exact Page Numbers Where You Find Information

Every time you note a fact or phrase from a print source, get down the page number because you will need to identify it in your paper.

Keep Your Notes Brief but Understandable

Take notes in phrases, not whole sentences. You will run yourself crazy if you try to take down every word, and your notes will be harder for you to read. If a quotation strikes you as important, copy it word for word and put quotation marks around it in your notes.

Downloading and Photocopying

Downloading is a real timesaver, but it increases the risk of plagiarism. Use a separate code name for each item copied electronically, and make sure that the file has all the publication information. Remember that every word of downloaded material is copied (plagiarized). This material cannot be used honestly in your own paper as is, but must be carefully quoted, paraphrased, or summarized, and documented.

When using a photocopy, you still must be able to tell where it came from; so immediately write the publication information on the photocopy.

In any case a photocopy or a copy to your disk is not a substitute for notes. When you take notes, you are taking a step toward putting the information you've found into your own words.

■ BALANCE RESEARCH AND WRITING

Write during Your Research

If you get an insight of your own as you are reading, stop and write about it. You may suddenly think of a great opening line, or realize that your points should come in a certain order, or disagree strongly with what you are reading. These ideas will evaporate if you don't write them down immediately. Later you may be able to expand them into parts of your paper.

Recognize Dead Ends

Rarely will you find anything useful on the second page of search results. Instead, rephrase the search.

Plan When to Stop Looking

Most students spend weeks gathering information and only days (or hours!) writing the report. Set a deadline for when you'll stop looking for more information.

◼ CAUTIONS FOR RESEARCH ON THE INTERNET

The Internet can take up all of your research time. If you're not careful, you can get lost—adding too many subtopics or switching to new topics until your project loses its shape.

Remember to bookmark. You may never be able to return to some sources you come across. Be methodical about adding "favorites" when using your own computer; when you're using another computer, email yourself each Internet address.

Be skeptical. Some very good information is posted informally. However, anyone can claim to be an authority, and widely repeated information is not necessarily accurate. Even accurate quotations or statistics, when taken out of context, can be presented in a misleading way. Above all, be careful not to get all of your data from a single report.

Finding information isn't the same as understanding it. Once you've found a good source, you have to read it patiently and take notes.

Getting Information Online
and at the Library

The library is your best single source of information. Nowadays you can use many of your college library's resources from your own computer. For other resources, such as books, you'll need to be physically inside the library.

However, the danger in both the Internet and the library is not knowing what you want and getting lost in the maze of research. To avoid getting lost, be sure to write down in advance the primary questions you hope to answer and some search terms you can use in your research.

■ Going beyond Google and *Wikipedia*

Most people rely on Google as their usual avenue onto the Web. As comprehensive as it is, however, Google won't list most magazine and newspaper articles relevant to your topic. For thorough research you should explore a variety of ways to find information. For descriptions and addresses of resources mentioned here, plus many others, see pages 187–90.

Wikipedia may be helpful as a starting point—it has the advantages of being written for the general public and being updated frequently; increasingly, its sources are referenced. However, many teachers will not accept *Wikipedia* as a legitimate source because anyone—not necessarily experts—can add or delete information, rendering some sections inaccurate.

FINDING ARTICLES USING SPECIALIZED DATABASES

Databases organized by subject will lead you to articles from scholarly journals and general sources such as the *New York Times* and *Newsweek*. Begin with the home page at your college library. Look for *FirstSearch* (which connects you to a variety of other databases), for databases in specific fields of study (such as *Medline* and *Findlaw*), or for *LexisNexis* (which indexes all news articles). Often you can read the entire article on your computer. Otherwise, make a list of the periodicals and pages you want, including the date. Usually the database will tell if your library has the article and where to find it.

Databases vary in size from a small glossary to an entire library. Some are available on the Web; for example, Google Scholar provides access to many articles in scholarly journals. However, some of the best databases are available only through your college library.

Government agencies and nonprofit organizations provide valuable statistics and other information through their websites. Many will be listed on your library's reference page, but you can also use a search engine and add "government" to your search terms. Look for websites with *.gov* or *.org* in their addresses.

News and entertainment organizations provide detailed information through their websites about a wide variety of topics. Some organizations include photo, audio, and video materials as well.

Use the "Advanced Search" Feature

Search programs for other databases are not as easy to use as Google, so you will need to choose your search terms carefully. Use quotation marks around phrases ("pizza sauce"), avoid words that could also refer to other topics, and double-check your spelling. Most search programs allow you to refine your search. Check the "advanced search tips" for directions on how to specify:

- Words that are near (within ten words of) each other. For example, articles having "nutritional" and "pizza" close together will most likely discuss the nutritional aspects of pizza.

- The root of a word followed by an asterisk (*) to find variations of the word. Asking for *nutri** will call up articles that include *nutrient(s), nutrition, nutritional, nutritionist(s),* or *nutritious.*

- Synonyms of your term

- A range of publication dates

- File formats—useful when searching for graphics, for example

- Links to similar websites

No search engine will allow you to specify all these variations; you may find it helpful to keep notes on which searches you have tried.

FINDING BOOKS

Your first step in finding a book is to search in the online catalog of your library. Books, media holdings, and reference materials are cataloged by author, title, and subject. At least in the beginning, you will be searching by subject. On the computer follow the system's instructions to see a "brief record," listing several books, or to see a "full record," giving detailed information about each book. Use a variety of general search terms. For example, you probably won't find a book entitled *The Nutritional Value of Pizza,* but you will find books including both of the subjects *pizza* and *nutrition.* When you find books that look valuable, copy down the catalog numbers you need, or have the computer print a list for you. You need the complete call number to locate a book. It also helps to copy down the author and title. Once you find the book on the shelf, take time to browse through that section for other relevant titles.

Many books are also available in part or entirely online. *The Bartleby Project* and others have scanned classics no longer under copyright. Enter the title into a search engine, or see pages 188–89 for a list of addresses.

◼ USING OTHER RESOURCES IN THE LIBRARY

Reference Section

Most professors do not consider encyclopedia and dictionary articles adequate sources for college research papers. Nevertheless, encyclopedias and specialized reference books are often the best place to start your research because they give you an overview of your subject. The reference section of the library also contains bibliographies, maps, atlases, and special collections of statistical information. Ask the librarian where to browse for your particular subject.

Periodicals Section

As you are searching online, you may encounter titles of articles that are available only in the library. In addition some older articles in newspapers, magazines, and journals—useful for historical topics—can't be found unless you consult indexes in bound volumes. The *Reader's Guide to Periodicals* lists all subjects covered in popular magazines. The *New York Times Index* and the *National Newspaper Index* list subjects covered in newspapers each year. Make a list of the periodicals and pages you want, including the date. You may need to check the holdings file— the list of periodicals your library carries. The article will be available in a bound volume, in a loose copy, on CD, DVD, microfilm, or microfiche.

Media Section

Slides, filmstrips, videos, recordings, computer programs, and so forth are housed in the media section and indexed in the library catalog.

Pamphlet File

Sometimes called the *vertical file* or *clip file*, the pamphlet file stores clippings and pamphlets. It is an especially good source of material pertaining to local areas such as your state or home town. You'll need to ask a librarian for access.

Interlibrary Loan

At your request and with enough time, your library can obtain copies of books and articles from other libraries.

WHEN YOU FIND TOO FEW OR TOO MANY SOURCES

The help line for the particular program you are using is your first resource when you're in a jam. Here are some other steps to take:

No Match for Your Request

- You may have misspelled one or more words— names, in particular.

- You may have used the wrong phrasing for that particular search engine. Check the help line.

- You may have submitted too narrow a search. Try generalizing a bit—for example, change the term *pizza, transfat* to *pizza, fat*.

- Give both the abbreviation and the full name, linked by *or* (*NIH* or *National Institutes of Health*).

- You may need to try a different search engine or database.

- The information may be there, but your computer cannot reach it at this time. Try later.

Too Many Listings

- Take a look at the first ten results to see whether they coincide at all with your topic. For instance, if your inquiry on pizza yielded thousands of articles, and the first ten are all about specific restaurants, you'll need to rephrase the search.

- If the first ten listings are on your topic, skim a few of them to extract more search terms.

WRITING THE RESEARCH PAPER

You've collected all sorts of information. You have a folder, maybe even a box, full of notes. Now you have to decide what to share with the reader. Are you going to just hand the reader the box? You need to decide what's most important to say.

■ WRITE A FIRST DRAFT

If you try to write your final paper in one draft, you put yourself under too much pressure to make everything perfect the first time around. A fast first draft actually saves you time.

Discover Your Own Perspective

After you have read and understood your sources, put your notes, books, and magazines aside to find your own position on your topic. Freewrite or list ideas until you know what you think. Try to reduce your central point to a single sentence—your preliminary thesis.

Organize Your Thoughts and Write a Quick First Draft

The trick to a good first draft is to write it without consulting your notes. That way your paper will be in your own style, and you will write only what is clear to you. Later you can consult your notes for facts and quotations to add to your initial draft.

Without looking at your sources or notes, develop a short informal outline. Put all the major points you plan to make into a logical arrangement. Avoid merely giving a part of your paper to each source you read; instead, give a part to each of the points you want to make.

Here are two possible plans.

The first plan focuses on a thesis you intend to prove:

- The general topic or issue and your thesis
- The evidence for and against your thesis (the main part of your paper)
- The importance or implications of your findings

The second plan focuses on the questions you posed and the answers you discovered:

- The question(s) you set out to answer

- The answers you found (the main part of your paper)

- The importance or implications of your findings

If your teacher asks for a formal outline, or if you prefer to line up all the details before writing, use the classic format shown on page 74. Start with your informal outline, and fill in only the details that fit into it and support your central ideas. Do not stuff in everything you found or lose your focus.

Write a draft of your entire paper. Do this also without consulting your notes or your sources, just from memory. Be sure to include a paragraph for each topic in your outline. Explain information as you understand it; don't check the details yet.

Don't try for fancy words and long sentences. Tell what you know, emphasizing in your own words what is most important.

Write to persuade. Remember that you have become an authority. Use the facts that you remember to back up your position. Anticipate the reader's questions and doubts, and respond to them ahead of time.

Four Concerns You Can Defer until Later

- The perfect introduction: Once you see how your paper comes out, you can go back and improve your introduction.

- Spelling and punctuation: Save this concern until the revision stage.

- Documentation: You will add this information to your second draft.

- Length: You don't have to aim for a certain length yet. When you have a full first draft, you'll begin to see where information and explanations are needed.

▨ INCORPORATE INFORMATION: QUOTATIONS, PARAPHRASE, SUMMARY, AND VISUALS

Once you have a first draft, you need to consult your notes. Read them and see which notes support the main points of your first draft. Be very selective. Disregard material that does not pertain to your main points—it will only distract or overwhelm your reader.

General Guidelines for Incorporating Information

- Don't download or copy hunks of information. Set your sources aside and write information in your own words.

- Don't overload your paragraphs with facts and quotations.

- Weave together several sources rather than using one source at a time.

- Lead into facts or quotations gracefully. Often it's most effective to use the name of the author in your sentence.

  > According to D. M. Larsen, ...
  > Regina Schrambling, in "Tex-Mex Pizza," tells how ...

- When you present a fact or quotation, relate it to the larger point you are making. In your own words clarify the importance of the fact or quotation.

- As you insert a fact, quotation, opinion, or visual from a source, note the author and the exact page where you found it. For APA documentation style, also note the copyright year.

Balance the three different ways of presenting information: *direct quotation, paraphrase,* and *summary.* In addition, computers now make it easy to include photographs, charts, and other helpful visuals.

Direct Quotation

In direct quotation you use the *exact* wording from your material and surround the words with quotation marks. Even if you use only a phrase or a key word, you must indicate that it has been taken from someone else by placing it within quotation marks. "Incorporating Quotations" (pages 82–83) gives strategies for using quotations. "Quotation Marks" (pages 44–47) will help you with the correct form for quotations.

Direct quotation is often overused in research papers.
Quotations should be secondary to your own ideas. Don't use
many quotations, and keep the ones you do use brief—three or
four lines at most. When you can, work a *phrase* from the author
into your own sentence. Your paper should not be more than
15 percent quotation.

- *Do quote:*

    ~ Memorable and distinctive phrases

    ~ Strong statements of opinion by authorities

- *Do not quote:*

    ~ Facts and statistics

    He was born in 1945.

    ~ Standard terminology in a field

    asthma   velocity

To avoid relying too heavily on quotation, make a point of
using the other two methods, paraphrase and summary.

Paraphrase

When you paraphrase, you take someone else's idea or
information and put it into your own words. Usually you
paraphrase one statement, not more than a few lines, at one
time. A good place for paraphrase, rather than quotation, is
in telling basic facts: dates, statistics, places, and so forth. The
pitfall in paraphrasing comes when you stick too closely to your
source's phrasing, writing things you don't fully understand in
language not really your own. Instead, read the passage, close
the book, and write your paraphrase in plain English.

You can't half paraphrase. That is, if you mix in some of the
author's exact words, you must use quotation marks around
them.

Summary

When you summarize, you take a substantial amount of
material and condense it. You can summarize a long passage,
several pages, a chapter, or even an entire article or book. Use
summary when you want to acknowledge a conflicting idea or
when you want to cover a related idea without too much detail.

POWERPOINT PRESENTATIONS

In some courses you may be reporting your research in PowerPoint.

For PowerPoint presentations, minimize text and give explanations orally. When your presentation is primarily visual, text should support, not distract. Write out only your main talking points. Use minimal phrases so that the viewer can focus on the image. You don't want your audience to still be reading the screen while you are talking about the next point.

Use enough visuals to illustrate your ideas. Use graphs, pie charts, drawings, photos, and color.

Avoid clutter. Make each visual big enough to be easily seen. Sometimes one large picture is much more effective than four tiny ones.

Make sure that the arrangement of your images is logical. Viewers naturally "read" images left to right, then top to bottom. Use arrows, zooms, or captions to draw attention to the features you want the viewer to notice.

Use brief captions to explain each image. Identify people, locations, or significant elements. (Your *Works Cited* page will give details for the sources of each image.)

Visuals

Visuals—charts, maps, drawings, photographs—can communicate a large amount of information in a small space.

- **Don't just stick in a visual for effect.** First be certain that the illustration gives additional information or clarifies a statement in your paper. It has to have a purpose beyond looking cute.

- **Be sure that your illustration is clear.** Enlarge it if you need to.

- **Give each visual a caption** and place it into the text right at the point where you have discussed it; however, if the visuals will be too disruptive to the paper, add them in an appendix at the end.

- **Give the source of the illustration if you did not create it.** (For proper documentation see pages 139 and 146.)

▓ PREPARE YOUR FINAL PAPER

First go through your paper to make sure every point is understandable. Add what you need to. Get rid of tangents and wordiness.

- Is every fact and quotation accurate?

- Have you led smoothly into your quotations, so the reader won't be confused about the person you are quoting or about the context?

- Have you put a citation after each fact, idea, quotation, or visual taken from a source?

- Do the citations match the first word of the corresponding entry in your *Works Cited* or *References* page?

- Have you proofread for errors and typos?

▓ A SAMPLE RESEARCH PAPER

To see the format, style, and documentation of a sample research paper, go to

http://www.mhhe.com/rules8e

where "Dirty Times," a study of changing notions of cleanliness, is reprinted just as it was written by a student, although some sources have been updated.

Plagiarism (Cheating)

Penalties for plagiarism can be severe: failure of the course or expulsion from the college. Unintentional plagiarism is still plagiarism, so be careful and know the rules.

Plagiarism means *writing facts, quotations, or opinions that you got from someone else without identifying your source; or using someone else's words without putting quotation marks around them.*

To Avoid Plagiarizing

- Always give credit for a fact, quotation, or opinion whether you read it, retrieved it electronically, saw it on television, heard it on the radio, or learned it from another person—even when you use your own wording.

- When you use another person's wording—even a phrase—always put quotation marks around the person's exact words.

- Write your first draft with your books closed. Do not write with a book, printout, or magazine open next to you. Don't go back and forth taking ideas from a source and writing your paper.

- Don't copy and paste downloaded material. Read it and then tell the point in your own words; if you wish to quote an exact phrase or sentence, put it in quotation marks. Either way—summarized or quoted—be sure to cite its source immediately following the summary or quotation. Give credit for any visuals as well.

- Don't let your sources take over the essay. Tell what you know well, in your own style, stressing what you find most important.

What Is Documentation?

The word *documentation* means that you have added two elements to your paper:

- In the body of your paper, right after you present information, you give a brief *citation* identifying the source of that information.

- At the end of your paper, you provide a separate page with a detailed list of your sources in alphabetical order. This list is called *Works Cited*, *References*, or *Bibliography*.

When to Give Your Source

You must acknowledge in your paper the source of

- A direct quotation

- A statistic

- An idea

- Someone else's opinion

- Concrete facts

- Illustrations, photographs, or charts—if not your own or if created from published materials

- Information not commonly known

Even if you paraphrase (put someone else's words into your own words) or summarize (condense someone else's words or ideas), you still must cite the source of your information.

On many websites you will notice a line from the author granting permission to reproduce the material for personal or educational use. However, you still have to give that author credit.

If a fact is common knowledge (George Washington was the first president), you don't have to give your source.

How Often to Give Your Source

When several facts in a row within one paragraph all come from the same page of a source, use one citation to cover them all. Place the citation after the last fact, but alert the reader at the outset with a phrase such as "According to Janet Tynan, …"

Do not, however, wait more than a few lines to let the reader know where the facts came from. The citation must be in the same paragraph as the facts.

Remember: You must give citations for information, not just for quotations.

How to Give Your Source

Different subject areas use different methods of documentation. Be sure to find out from your professor which method is preferable for that subject. Three basic styles of documentation are used most frequently. They all employ similar formats for the list of sources at the end of the paper, but they differ in the format they use for citations in the body of the paper:

- MLA (Modern Language Association)—used in English and literature courses (pages 136–49)

- APA (American Psychological Association)—used in the natural sciences and social sciences (pages 150–58)

- Footnotes or Endnotes—used in journalism, art, and history courses (pages 159–62)

The following chapters present these three styles.

WHERE TO FIND SPECIFIC ENTRIES FOR *WORKS CITED, REFERENCES,* AND *BIBLIOGRAPHY**

Type of Source		Documentation Style	
		MLA	APA*
Book		141	155
Article	found online or in library database	143	155–56
	in magazine	142	155
	in newspaper	142	155
	in scholarly journal	143	155–56
	in anthology	143	155
Author	none listed	144	153
	two or more	144	153
	quoted by someone else	138	151
Website		142	151, 156
Blog or Posting		144	157
Email		143	152
Encyclopedia		144	157
Illustration or Graphic		146	
Interview, Speech, or Lecture		146	152
Missing Information		147	
Pamphlet		145	155
Television or Radio		145	
Video or Audio Recording		145	

*For types of sources not included in the chapter on APA style, adapt the MLA details to the general format you are using. For a *Bibliography*, follow the format for *Works Cited* in MLA style.

DOCUMENTATION: THE MLA STYLE

HOW TO USE PARENTHETICAL CITATION

The MLA (Modern Language Association) style of documentation is used for courses in English and in foreign languages.

MLA style uses *parenthetical citation*. In this system you give your source in parentheses immediately after you give the information. Your reader can then find the complete listing of each source at the end of the paper in your *Works Cited* section.

The four most common citations are

- Author and page number
- Title and page number
- Page number only
- Secondhand quotations

For any citation it is crucial that the first word of the citation match the first word of the corresponding entry on your *Works Cited* page in the back of your paper.

Author and Page Number

Put the author's last name and the page number in parentheses immediately after the information:

```
(Levine 54)
```

Notice that there is no "p." and no comma. In the text it looks like this:

```
Pizza chains began with Pizza Hut in 1958
(Levine 54).
```

If your citation comes at the end of a sentence, the period goes outside the last parenthesis. (Exception: With indented quotations, the period goes before the parenthesis.)

Title and Page Number

Often articles, editorials, pamphlets, and other materials have no author listed. In such cases give only the first distinctive words of the title followed by the page number:

> The actual fat content of a frozen pizza may be
> more than the package claims ("A Meal" 19).

Note that you give the title of the specific article that you read, not the title of the newspaper, magazine, or reference book ("A Meal," not *Consumer Reports*).

Page Number Only

Put only the page number in parentheses when you have already mentioned the author's name.

> Ed Levine notes that "The appeal of pizza crosses
> all ethnic, racial and class lines" (10).

When possible, use this method of citation. Mentioning the author's name as you present information makes your paper more cohesive and readable.

No Page Number Available

For most electronic sources, no page number is given. The best option is simply to mention the author or title in your sentence.

> Hanna Miller reports that 93% of Americans eat
> pizza at least once a month.

If a parenthetical citation is more graceful, include the author, if given—otherwise the title.

> Ninety-three percent of Americans eat pizza at
> least once a month (Miller).

Sometimes electronic sources use section numbers; treat them like page numbers.

Secondhand Quotations

When you quote someone who has been quoted in one of your sources, use *qtd. in* (quoted in):

> Patrick Doyle, Domino's executive vice-president
> for international operations, says that pizza
> "plays incredibly well with really every cultural
> and regional and demographic group" (qtd. in
> Crossette 2).

In this example Doyle said it, although you found it in Crossette. Note that Doyle will not be listed in your *Works Cited*; Crossette will be.

However, whenever possible, go to the original source to verify the quotation, and then quote it directly.

SPECIAL CASES

Organization as Author Sometimes the author is an organization.

> According to the United States Department of
> Agriculture, one slice of cheese pizza has
> 255 calories (1).

or

> One slice of cheese pizza has 255 calories
> (United States Dept. of Agriculture 1).

Note: Do not abbreviate in your sentence—only in the parenthetical citation.

Two Sources by the Same Author When you have two or more sources by the same author, use the first identifying words to indicate the title of the work you're citing.

> Julia Child advises that the dough be chilled to
> slow the rising (*In Julia's* 6).

or

> Some chefs chill the dough to slow the rising
> (Child, *In Julia's* 6).

Interview, Speech, or Broadcast If your source is an interview, lecture, or speech, include the person's name and position in your paragraph and use no parenthetical citation.

> Kevin O'Reilly, owner of K. O'Reilly's Pizza, reports that pepperoni pizza outsells the low-fat versions ten to one.

> Professor Carlo Mangoni, who teaches nutrition at the Second University of Naples, said in a radio interview that there are only two classic pizzas— the marinara and the margherita.

Illustration or Graphics Citations for illustrations and graphics go in parentheses below the graphic.

- If the artist is identified, give the last name and page number.

> (Stevens 63)

- If the artist is not identified (for instance, in an advertisement) give the product name (or owner of the copyright) and page where the illustration appeared.

> (Kraft Foods 5)

SAMPLE PARAGRAPH USING CITATIONS

The following paragraph is a sample in which you can see how various citations are used. (You will rarely have this many citations in one short paragraph.) The sources cited here can be found among the works cited on page 149.

> When the first pizzeria opened in New York City in 1905, it introduced the classic Italian pizza—bread dough covered with tomato sauce and cheese ("Pizza" 490). Now, more than a century later, the American pizza reflects this country's love of diversity. In addition to the classic version, pizza lovers can now savor just about every combination and concoction imaginable. The National Association of Pizza Operators reports that

> Pizza makers have tried virtually every type
> of food on pizzas, including peanut butter and
> jelly, bacon and eggs, and mashed potatoes.
> (qtd. in "A Meal" 21)

The whole world has influenced American pizza. For
example, Evelyne Slomon calls Latino pizza the latest
"major movement," reflecting influences from every Hispanic
country. From France comes the pissaladière, which
adds fresh herbs, black olives, and anchovies (Child,
Bertholle, and Beck 151). There is even pizza topped with
Indian curry or Korean pickled cabbage (Levine 62). You
might have to travel to Italy to get authentic Italian
pizza; but you can eat your way across this country—and
the world—sampling several hundred modern versions of
pizza made the American way.

■ WORKS CITED

When you were gathering your material, you may have used
a "working bibliography," a list of potential sources. However,
now that you have written your paper and have seen which
sources you actually did use, you must include a separate page
at the end of the paper listing your *Works Cited*.

There are five major points to understand about a *Works Cited*
page:

- List *only* those sources that you actually referred to in your
  paper.

- *Alphabetize* your list of sources by the authors' last names. If no
  author is listed, alphabetize by the first main word in the title.

- List the whole article, essay, or book—not just the pages you
  used.

- MLA now requires that you indicate the format of the source you used—Web (with date viewed), Print, DVD, and so forth.

- Format is extremely important to many teachers. Pay special attention to order, spacing, and punctuation.

  ~ Put the author's last name first.

  ~ Double-space the entire list.

  ~ Start each entry at the left margin.

  ~ Indent the second and following lines of each entry five spaces ("hanging indent").

  ~ Notice that most of the items in a citation are separated by periods.

  ~ Italicize titles of books, periodicals, and websites; place quotation marks around titles of articles, chapters, and individual sections of websites.

  ~ For online sources, give the Web address (URL) only if necessary to find the source, and then as briefly as possible. (If you can google the title, you don't need the URL.) Enclose the URL in angle brackets: <http://tinyurl.com/8mayv>.

  ~ Leave one space after a comma, colon, or period.

  ~ Put a period at the end of each entry.

Examples of the format for specific entries follow. A sample *Works Cited* appears on page 149.

SPECIFIC ENTRIES

If complete information about your source is not available—for example, the name of the author—just list whatever information you have, in the order given below, without blank spaces.

Book

Author. *Title*. City: Publisher, date. Format.

```
Love, Louise. The Complete Book of Pizza.
        Evanston, IL: Sassafras, 1980. Print.
```

Note: If the city of publication is not well known, give the two-letter Post Office abbreviation for the state, without periods.

MLA

Website

Author or organization. "Title of Section, if given." *Title of the Website.* Sponsoring organization or publisher. Date of publication or last revision. Web. Date you viewed it.

> Slomon, Evelyne. "Viva Latino Pizza!" *PMQ.* Pizza
> Marketing Quarterly, Apr.-May 2006. Web.
> 20 Mar. 2009.

Note: Abbreviate all months except May, June, and July.

Article in a Magazine

Author. "Title of Article." *Title of Periodical* Date: page(s). Format.

> Miller, Hanna. "American Pie: How a Neapolitan Street
> Food Became the Most Successful Immigrant of All."
> *American Heritage* Apr.-May 2006: 30+. Print.

Note: When an article covers more than one page, use a comma to join two sequential numbers (36, 37) or a hyphen to join the first and last of more than two continuous numbers (36–39); otherwise, use + (36+).

If you found the article online, follow the directions for a website.

> Miller, Hanna. "American Pie: How a Neapolitan Street
> Food Became the Most Successful Immigrant of
> All." *American Heritage.com.* American Heritage,
> Apr.-May 2006. Web. 20 Mar. 2009.

Article in a Newspaper

Author (if given). "Title of Article." *Title of Newspaper* Complete date, name of edition if given, section number or title: page(s) if given. Format.

> Crossette, Barbara. "Burgers Are the Globe's Fast
> Food? Not So Fast." *New York Times* 26 Nov.
> 2000, New York ed., sec.4:2. Print.

If you found the article online, follow the directions for a website.

Article or Story in a Collection or Anthology

Author of article. "Title of Article." *Title of Book*. Editor of book. City: Publisher, date. Pages covered by article. Format.

> Heimburger, Douglas C. "Nutrients: Metabolism,
>
> Requirements, and Sources." *Handbook of*
>
> *Clinical Nutrition*. Ed. Douglas C. Heimburger
>
> and Jamy Ard. 4th ed. Philadelphia: Mosby-
>
> Elsevier, 2006. 44-137. Print.

Article in a Scholarly Journal

Author. "Title of Article." *Title of Journal* Volume number. Issue number (Year): pages covered by article. Format. Date viewed if online.

> Larsen, D. M., et al. "The Effects of Flour
>
> Type and Dough Retardation Time on Sensory
>
> Characteristics of Pizza Crust." *Cereal*
>
> *Chemistry* 70.6 (1993): 647-50. Print.

Article Originally in Print Found through Library Computer System

Information for print version (see above). Information service. Web. Date viewed.

> Hickman, Martin. "Fast-Food 'Healthy Options' Still
>
> Full of Fat and Salt." *Independent* [London]
>
> 1 Dec. 2005. LexisNexis. Web. 20 Mar. 2009.

Direct E-mail to You (Not a Discussion Group)

Author of email. "Subject line." Message to the author (meaning you). Date. E-mail.

> Brooks, Evelyn. "Re: Pizza." Message to the author.
>
> 10 Mar. 2009. E-mail.

Note that MLA still prefers the spelling "e-mail."

Blog or Discussion Group

Name of author. "Title [or subject line of posting]." *Title of Blog or Discussion Group*. Publisher. Date posted. Web. Date viewed.

> Kuban, Adam. "A List of Regional Pizza Styles."
> *Serious Eats*. Serious Eats. 24 Jan. 2008.
> Web. 20 Mar. 2009.

Encyclopedia

"Title of Article." *Title of Encyclopedia*. Publisher, Year. Web. Date viewed.

> "Pizza." *Encyclopaedia Britannica Online*.
> Encyclopaedia Britannica, 2009. Web. 18 Mar.
> 2009.

For print versions give the number of the edition. Year. Print.

> "Pizza." *Encyclopaedia Britannica*. 15th ed. 2007.
> Print.

For less well-known encyclopedias, include the publisher's information, as for a book.

SPECIAL CASES

No Author Listed Alphabetize according to the first main word of the title. Include *A, An, The,* but do not use them when alphabetizing. For example, this article will be alphabetized with *M* in the *Works Cited:*

> "A Meal That's Easy as Pie: How to Pick a Pizza
> That's Good and Healthful." *Consumer Reports*
> Jan. 1997: 19-23. Print.

Two or More Authors Give the last name first for the first author only; use first name first for the other author(s).

> Child, Julia, Louisette Bertholle, and Simone Beck.
> *Mastering the Art of French Cooking*. Vol. 1.
> New York: Knopf, 1966. Print.

For four or more authors, list the first author, and then put et al. (meaning "and others").

Additional Works by the Same Author Use three hyphens and a period in place of the author's name and alphabetize the works by title.

> Child, Julia. *From Julia Child's Kitchen*. New York:
>
> Knopf, 1979. Print.
>
> ---. *In Julia's Kitchen with Master Chefs*. New
>
> York: Knopf, 1995. Print.

Pamphlet Follow the format for a book. Often an organization is the publisher. If no author is listed, begin with the title. If no date is listed, use n.d. for no date.

> United States Dept. of Agriculture. *Eating Better*
>
> *When Eating Out: Using the Dietary Guidelines*.
>
> Washington: GPO, n.d. Print.

Television or Radio Program Name of speaker. "Title of the Episode" (if available). *Title of the Program.* Network, if any. Station call letters, City. Date of the broadcast. Format.

> Brown, Alton. "Flat Is Beautiful." *Good Eats*.
>
> Food Network. WFTV, New York. 23 May 2006.
>
> Television.

Video or Audio Recording—Film, DVD, CD, MP3 File, etc. *Title.* Author, director, or performer. Distributor. Release date. Format.

Use abbreviations to indicate the function of any individuals you have discussed.

> *Mystic Pizza*. Dir. Donald Petrie. Scr. Amy Holden
>
> Jones. Perf. Annabeth Gish, Julia Roberts,
>
> Lili Taylor. MGM. 1988. DVD.

If you have discussed an individual's work, rather than the entire performance, list that name before the title.

> Smith, Jeff, perf. and writ. *Frugal Gourmet: Sauces*
>
> *and Seasonings—Garlic! Garlic!* MPI Home
>
> Video, 1992. Videocassette.

Interview, Speech, or Lecture Name [position]. Kind of presentation (type of interview, speech, or classroom lecture). Location. Date.

> O'Reilly, Kevin [Owner, K. O'Reilly's Pizza].
>> Personal interview. Troy, MO. 21 Mar. 2009.

If the speech is available as a transcript or recording, give the information as for a website.

> Nestle, Marion. "How the Food Industry Influences
>> Diet and Health." *5th Annual Rhoda Goldman*
>> *Distinguished Lecture in Health Policy.* U of
>> California Berkeley, 1 Apr. 2003. Web. 20
>> Mar. 2009.

Illustration or Graphics

- If your paper includes photographs or illustrations that you have created, add a parenthetical citation directly below the graphic in your paper (Photo by Author) or (Chart by Author). Do not include a credit in your *Works Cited.*

- If the image was created by someone else, give the artist's name if known or the company name (for example, for an advertisement). Give the title for the image in quotation marks; otherwise, indicate the type of image (for example, cartoon or photograph). Then give the information for the source that contains the illustration.

> Stevens, Mick. Cartoon. *New Yorker* 8 June 1992: 63.
>> Print.

> Eden Foods. Advertisement. *Eating Well* July/Aug.
>> 2006: 13. Print.

> United States Dept. of Agriculture. "Food Guide
>> Pyramid." *Dietary Guidelines for Americans.*
>> Apr. 2005. Web. 21 Mar. 2009.

Missing Information

Use the following abbreviations to denote missing information:

no date of publication given	n.d.
no place of publication or no publisher	n.p.
no page numbers	n. pag.

The abbreviation goes where the information would have gone.

■ SAMPLE WORKS CITED PAGE

The *Works Cited* page on page 149 illustrates a variety of sources and therefore is longer than you probably will need. The left-hand page identifies the category of each source.

MLA

Explanations of Works Cited

Book, single author ————————————————————➤

Repeated author (same author as above) ——————————➤

Book, three authors, one volume cited (repeated author with
first citing of co-authors) —————————————————➤

Newspaper article ——————————————————————➤

Article or chapter in an edited collection [Use this form also for
a single selection from an anthology.] —————————————➤

Article originally in print found through library computer
service ———————————————————————————➤

Article in a scholarly journal, more than three authors ————➤

Book, single author ———————————————————————➤

Magazine article (monthly), unsigned ——————————————➤

Encyclopedia article, unsigned ———————————————————➤

Magazine article, online ——————————————————————➤

Works Cited

Child, Julia. *From Julia Child's Kitchen*. New York:
Knopf, 1979. Print.

---. *In Julia's Kitchen with Master Chefs*. New York:
Knopf, 1995. Print.

Child, Julia, Louisette Bertholle, and Simone Beck.
Mastering the Art of French Cooking. Vol. 1. New
York: Knopf, 1966. Print.

Crossette, Barbara. "Burgers Are the Globe's Fast Food?
Not So Fast." *New York Times*. New York Times,
26 Nov. 2000. Web. 18 Mar. 2009.

Heimburger, Douglas C. "Nutrients: Metabolism,
Requirements, and Sources." *Handbook of Clinical
Nutrition*. Ed. Douglas C. Heimburger and Jamy Ard.
4th ed. Philadelphia: Mosby-Elsevier, 2006. 44-137.
Print.

Hickman, Martin. "Fast-Food 'Healthy Options' Still Full
of Fat and Salt." *Independent* [London] 1 Dec. 2005.
LexisNexis. Web. 20 Mar. 2009.

Larsen, D. M., et al. "The Effects of Flour Type and
Dough Retardation Time on Sensory Characteristics of
Pizza Crust." *Cereal Chemistry* 70.6 (1993): 647-50.
Print.

Levine, Ed. *Pizza: A Slice of Heaven*. New York: Universe,
2005. Print.

"A Meal That's Easy as Pie: How to Pick a Pizza That's
Good and Healthful." *Consumer Reports* Jan. 1997:
19-23. Print.

"Pizza." *Encyclopaedia Britannica Online*. Encyclopaedia
Britannica. 2009. Web. 18 Mar. 2009.

Slomon, Evelyne. "Viva Latino Pizza!" *PMQ*. Pizza
Marketing Quarterly, Apr.-May 2006. Web.
20 Mar. 2009.

DOCUMENTATION: THE APA STYLE

The APA (American Psychological Association) style is used for courses in the social sciences, such as psychology, sociology, anthropology, and economics, and for some of the life sciences (consult your professor).

APA documentation style places the last name of the author and the year of publication in parentheses immediately after any research information. At the end of the paper, a complete list of sources (*References*) provides the details about the particular books, articles, and other documents you used.

For a sample paper and directions for formatting in the APA style, go to http://www.apastyle.org and click on APA Style Help.

■ PARENTHETICAL CITATIONS

Here are the most common forms for APA style:

For Books and Articles: Author and Year of Publication

The preferred form is to use the author's last name in your sentence, followed by the year of publication in parentheses:

    Levine (2005) described the universal appeal of

    pizza.

Note that in APA style, the author's work is referred to in the past tense ("described").

When the author is not mentioned in your sentence, the parentheses will contain both the author's last name and the year of publication.

    Pizza chains began with Pizza Hut in 1958 (Levine,

    2005).

If no author is listed, give only the first distinctive word of the title, followed by the year of publication. Give the title of the specific article that you read, in quotation marks, not the title of the newspaper, magazine, or reference book.

> America's pizza business began in 1905 ("Pizza,"
> 2008).

For Direct Quotations or Paraphrases: Page or Paragraph Number

When you have quoted or paraphrased, give the print page number (p. or pp.) or electronic paragraph number (para.) after the year. When an electronic source uses headings, give the number of the paragraph under that heading. Name the heading as a section or quote the first few distinctive words of a long heading.

> Di Laurentiis (2006, p. 240) described. . . .
>
> An Australian study found . . . (Malouf &
> Colagiuri, 1995, Discussion section, para. 8).
>
> Researchers discovered . . . (Stroebele & De
> Castro, 2004, "Meal Times," para. 2).

For Secondhand Quotations

When you quote or paraphrase someone who has been quoted in one of your sources, use *as cited in:*

> Domino's executive vice-president Doyle said that
> pizza "plays incredibly well with really every
> cultural and regional and demographic group" (as
> cited in Crossette, 2000, para. 3).

In this example, Doyle said it, but you found it in Crossette. Note that you will list Crossette in your references, not Doyle.

SPECIAL CASES

Websites When you have used an entire website as a general reference, refer to the website in your sentence and give its address in parentheses, but don't list it in *References:*

> The Fast Food Nutrition Fact Explorer posted
> nutritional data for the major pizza brands
> (http://www.fatcalories.com).

Personal Communications (Emails, Interviews, Lectures) When your source communicated with you personally, write, in parentheses, the words "personal communication" and the date (month day, year), but don't list it in *References*:

> O'Reilly, owner of K. O'Reilly's Pizza, reported that pepperoni pizza outsells the low-fat versions ten to one (personal communication, July 20, 2009).

More Than One Author For **two authors,** join the last names with *and* if you refer to them in your sentence or with an ampersand (&) if you cite them in parentheses. For **three to six authors,** give all the names for the first reference. Thereafter, use only the last name of the first author plus *et al.* (meaning "and others"). For **more than six authors,** give only the last name of the first author plus *et al.*

Two Sources by the Same Author When you have two or more sources by one author, the different dates will indicate the different sources. When two sources by the same author have the same date, put a lowercase letter after the year to distinguish the source—Jones 1994a, Jones 1994b, and so on. Use the alphabetical order of the titles to assign letters.

SAMPLE PARAGRAPH USING CITATIONS

In the following paragraph, you can see how various citations are used. (You will rarely have this many citations in one short paragraph.) The sources cited here can be found among the references on page 158.

> When the first pizzeria opened in New York City in 1905, it introduced the classic Italian pizza—bread dough covered with tomato sauce and cheese ("Pizza," 2009). Now, more than a century later, the simple pizza has been transformed into an American creation that reflects this country's love of diversity. In addition to the classic version, pizza lovers can now savor just about every combination and concoction imaginable. The National Association of Pizza Operators reported that "Pizza makers have tried virtually every type of food

on pizzas, including peanut butter and jelly, bacon and eggs, and mashed potatoes" (as cited in "A meal," 1997, p. 21). The whole world has influenced American pizza. For example, Slomon (2006) called Latino pizza the latest "major movement," reflecting influences from every Hispanic country. From France comes the pissaladière, which adds fresh herbs, black olives, and anchovies (Child, Bertholle, & Beck, 1966, p. 151). There is even pizza topped with Indian curry or Korean pickled cabbage (Levine, 2005). You might have to travel to Italy to get authentic Italian pizza; but you can eat your way across this country—and the world—sampling several hundred modern versions of pizza made the American way.

Note that APA uses two spaces after a period ending a sentence.

■ REFERENCES

At the end of your paper, on a separate page, list the sources that were mentioned in your paper or cited in parentheses. For the basic rules of Reference pages, see the section on "Works Cited" in the chapter on the MLA style of documentation, page 140. In addition, the following rules apply:

Heading

The list is titled *References*. It should be centered, capitalizing only the first letter, with no italics, underline, boldface, or quotation marks.

Authors' Names

- Alphabetize the list by authors' last names. Give only the initials for the first and middle names of authors. Give all names in reverse order. List all authors up to seven. With more than seven authors, list the first six and then add an ellipsis (three spaced periods) plus the last author's name.

- For authors who have written more than one work, repeat the name for each entry. List the works in chronological order. Alphabetize titles with the same date, adding a letter to the date—2000a, 2000b, and so on.

- If no author is listed, begin your entry with the title (but alphabetize by the first main word—not *The, A,* or *An*).

Date of Publication

Place the date of publication for each entry within parentheses right after the author's name (or after the title if no author is listed). For articles in a magazine or newspaper, include the year and month (not abbreviated). Add the day when given. Use n.d. for "no date."

Titles

- Capitalize only the first word of most titles and subtitles, but capitalize all main words of titles of newspapers, magazines, and scholarly journals.

- Use *italics* for the titles of books, newspapers, magazines, websites, albums, films, television programs, and podcasts. Titles of shorter works that appear inside larger ones—such as articles, chapters, Web postings—are printed without underlines, italics, or quotation marks.

- Use square brackets [ ] to insert a clarification after a title— such as [Video], [Online exclusive], [Web log message].

Publication Information

- Give the city of publication plus the US Postal Service abbreviation for the state unless the publisher's name includes it; give the city and country for foreign publications.

- When the author is also the publisher, write Author in place of the publisher's name.

- Do not abbreviate the names of book publishers; however, use & (ampersand) instead of "and." Include "Books," "University," and "Press," but omit "Co.," "Inc.," or "Publisher."

- Wherever possible, APA prefers citing the latest online versions of articles, because they are easier to access and may include corrections or additional information. Give the print publication information first, including page numbers and DOI. Give the Web address of the publisher's home page only if no DOI is available.

- When citing materials subject to change, such as wikis, add the date you retrieved the information.

- Use "retrieved from" and the URL where the document can be read. Use "available from" with the URL where the document can be downloaded.

- Include the prefix (such as http or ftp), but then give the shortest URL that will allow your reader to find the information. Do not end the URL or accession number with a period.

SPECIFIC ENTRIES

Book or Pamphlet

Author. (Year). *Title*. City, State: Publisher.

> De Laurentiis, G. (2006). *Giada's family dinners*.
> New York, NY: Clarkson Potter.

Article in a Collection or Anthology

Author of article. (Year). Title of article. In Editor of book (Ed.), *Title of book* (pages covered by article). City: Publisher.

> Heimburger, D. C. (2006). Nutrients: Metabolism,
> requirements, and sources. In D. C.
> Heimburger & J. Ard (Eds.), *Handbook of
> clinical nutrition* (4th ed., pp. 44-137).
> Philadelphia, PA: Mosby-Elsevier.

Article in a Newspaper

Author. (Complete date, year first). Title of article. *Title of Periodical*, Sec. [for section if needed], p. or pp. [pages covered].

> Crossette, B. (2000, November 26). Burgers are the
> globe's fast food? Not so fast. *The New York
> Times*, Sec. 4, p. 2.

See page 158 for the format for a newspaper article online.

Article in a Scholarly Journal or Magazine

Author. (Year). Title of article. *Title of Journal, Volume number*(issue number), pages covered by article, doi: (Digital Object Identifier—if available, the number above or below the abstract of the scholarly article)

> Ferrara, L. A., Pacioni, D., Vitolo, G., Staiano,
> L., Riccio, E., & Gaetano, G. (2008). Fast
> food versus slow food and hypertension
> control. *Current Hypertension Reviews, 4*(1),
> 30-36. doi: 10.2174/157340208783497219

If no DOI is given, and you read the article online, add "Retrieved from" and the URL for the journal's home page—even if you found the article through a library database. (Do not list the URL if you have given the DOI number.)

> Worth the dough. (2005, March). *Men's Health,
> 20*(2), 46. Retrieved from http://www.
> menshealth.com

Specific Document on a Website

Author or organization (if known). (Date of publication or last revision). Title of the article. *Title of the Complete Work.* Retrieved date from address of the website

> Harvard School of Public Health. (2009). Protein.
> *Nutrition Source.* Retrieved March 20,
> 2009, from http://www.hsph.harvard.edu/
> nutritionsource

Entire Website—see "Websites," page 151.

Personal Communication (Interview, Speech, Lecture, or Email)—see "Personal Communications," page 152.

Encyclopedia

Author of article if given. (Date). Title of article. In *Title of encyclopedia.* Retrieved from Web address

```
Pizza. (2009). In Encyclopaedia Britannica.
     Retrieved from http://www.britannica.com/
     EBchecked/topic/462475/pizza
```

Posting to a Blog or Discussion Group

Name of author. (Date of the posting). Re: Subject line of the message. [Online Forum Comment *or* Web log message]. Message posted to name of group (if needed), Web address

```
diogenes. (2007, April 10). Re: Who pays $731 for a
     pizza? [Online Forum Comment]. Message posted
     to http://freakonomics.dblogs.nytimes.com/
```

The following page includes the references for the sample paragraph on pages 152–53.

APA

References

Child, J. (1995). *In Julia's kitchen with master chefs.* New York, NY: Knopf.

Child, J. (2000). *Julia's kitchen wisdom: Essential techniques and recipes from a lifetime of cooking.* New York, NY: Knopf.

Child, J., Bertholle, L., & Beck, S. (1966). *Mastering the art of French cooking* (Vol. 1). New York, NY: Knopf.

Crossette, B. (2000, November 26). Burgers are the globe's fast food? Not so fast. *The New York Times.* Retrieved from http://www.nytimes.com

Ferrara, L. A., Pacioni, D., Vitolo, G., Staiano, L., Riccio, E., & Gaetano, G. (2008). Fast food versus slow food and hypertension control. *Current Hypertension Reviews, 4*(1), 30-36. doi: 10.2174/157340208783497219

Harvard School of Public Health. (2007). Protein. *Nutrition Source.* Retrieved July 20, 2009, from http://www.hsph.harvard.edu/nutritionsource

Heimburger, D. C. (2006). Nutrients: Metabolism, requirements, and sources. In D. C. Heimburger & J. Ard (Eds.), *Handbook of clinical nutrition* (4th ed., pp. 44-137). Philadelphia, PA: Mosby-Elsevier.

Levine, E. (2005). *Pizza: A slice of heaven.* New York, NY: Universe.

A meal that's easy as pie: How to pick a pizza that's good and healthful. (1997, January). *Consumer Reports, 62,* 19-23.

Pizza. (2009). In *Encyclopaedia Britannica.* Retrieved from http://www.britannica.com/EBchecked/topic/462475/pizza

DOCUMENTATION: FOOTNOTES, ENDNOTES, AND BIBLIOGRAPHY

This traditional system is the best choice for courses in art, business, communications, dance, journalism, law, music, theater, history, or political science; for cross-disciplinary courses; and for a general audience.

■ CONTENT NOTES

When you have supplementary information but don't want to clutter the body of your paper, you may include it in a note—either at the bottom of the page (footnote) or at the end of your paper (endnote). Doing so is acceptable when using MLA or APA style. Use a raised (superscript) number in your sentence to direct the reader to the information. Word processing makes this easy to do.[1]

■ SOURCE NOTES

Some teachers in certain disciplines prefer the use of footnotes or endnotes for all citations of sources.

Here are the basic formats for citing books, articles, and websites:

• Place the footnote number immediately after the fact or quotation it documents.

• The number in your text is raised (superscript), but the corresponding number in the footnote is in normal font followed by a period.

• The numbers for footnotes are continuous; that is, you begin with the number 1 and progress, using the next number each time you document a fact or quotation from your research.

• Omit the author's name in the footnote if you have already mentioned it in your paragraph.

---

1. For example, click Insert>Reference>Footnote, then select the format you wish.

Book

1. Author's first and last names, *Title of Book* (City: Publisher, Date), page(s) cited.

Article in a Magazine or Newspaper

2. Author's first and last names [if given], "Title of Article," *Title of Magazine* or *Newspaper* (Day Month Year): page(s) or <Web address>.

Article in a Scholarly Journal

3. Author's first and last names, "Title of Article," *Title of Scholarly Journal*, Volume number. Issue number (Year): pages or <Web address> or Library Service (such as InfoTrac).

Website

4. Author's first and last names or Sponsoring Organization [if given],"Title of Article or Section," *Title of Website*, Date of last update, <Web address> (date accessed).

For other types of sources, follow the directions for the MLA *Works Cited* (pages 140–49), but do not reverse the author's names, and use different punctuation as shown in the examples in this chapter. Give the briefest Web address (URL) possible, or go to http://TinyUrl.com for a short URL to use. Do not specify "Print" or "Web" in your footnotes or endnotes, but do specify DVD or other specialized formats.

After the first complete footnote, subsequent footnotes for that source give only the last name of the author (or a short form of the title if no author is given) and the appropriate page number.

5. Louise Love, *The Complete Book of Pizza* (Evanston, IL: Sassafras, 1980), 35.
6. Love, 38.

Word processing programs can automatically format the notes and keep track of your sequence of numbers during both composition and revision.

Here is an example of a paragraph using footnotes. Check the numerals and the matching footnotes at the bottom of the page:

When the first pizzeria opened in New York City in 1905, it introduced the classic Italian pizza—bread dough covered with tomato sauce and cheese.[1] Now, more than a century later, the simple pizza has been transformed into an American creation that reflects this country's love of diversity. In addition to the classic version, pizza lovers can now savor just about every combination and concoction imaginable. The National Association of Pizza Operators reports:

> Pizza makers have tried virtually every type of food on pizzas, including peanut butter and jelly, bacon and eggs, and mashed potatoes.[2]

The whole world has influenced American pizza. For example, Evelyne Slomon calls Latino pizza the latest "major movement," reflecting influences from every Hispanic country.[3] From France comes the pissaladière, which adds fresh herbs, black olives, and anchovies.[4] There is even pizza topped with Indian curry or Korean pickled cabbage.[5] You might have to travel to Italy to get authentic Italian pizza; but you can eat your way across this country—and the world—sampling several hundred modern versions of pizza made the American way.

---

1. "Pizza," *Encyclopaedia Britannica Online*, 2009 (18 Mar. 2009).

2. Qtd. in "A Meal That's Easy as Pie: How to Pick a Pizza That's Good and Healthful," *Consumer Reports* (Jan. 1997): 19–23.

3. "Viva Latino Pizza!" *PMQ [Pizza Marketing Quarterly]* (Apr.–May 2006), <http://www.pmq.com/> (20 Mar. 2009).

4. Julia Child, Louisette Bertholle, and Simone Beck, *Mastering the Art of French Cooking*, vol. 1 (New York: Knopf, 1966), 151.

5. Ed Levine, *Pizza: A Slice of Heaven* (New York: Universe, 2005), 62.

■ FORMAT FOR ENDNOTES

Endnotes are listed in numerical order at the end of the paper on a separate page, called *Notes*. Use the same format as for footnotes, and double-space the entire page.

■ SHORT FORM FOR FOOTNOTES AND ENDNOTES

When you use a bibliography, your footnotes or endnotes can simply give the author's last name and page number (if available). If no author is listed, give a brief form of the title.

■ BIBLIOGRAPHY

At the end of the paper, a bibliography lists all the sources referred to in the notes. Each source is listed only once—in alphabetical order by the authors' last names (not in the order you used them) and in the same format as for *Works Cited* in MLA style (see pages 140–49). Title your list *Bibliography*—using cap/lowercase, without italics, underline, boldface, or quotation marks.

In addition, this system allows for a *Supplementary Bibliography*—a list of sources that you have read for background or tangential information but did not actually refer to in the report.

The bibliography for the sample paragraph on pages 160–61 would follow the format of the MLA *Works Cited* on page 149, except that it would be called *Bibliography*.

PART 4

STYLE

FINDING YOUR VOICE

When we write the way we think we're supposed to, with big words and fancy sentences, the writing comes out awkward and impersonal. But good writing has the feel of a real person explaining the subject. You don't have to use slang; just write in a clear, friendly style.

To find your own voice as a writer, keep these questions in mind when you write:

Am I saying this in plain English?

Are these words that I normally use?

Am I saying what I know to be true instead of what I think others want to hear?

A great technique for developing your own voice is to read your work aloud. If you do it regularly, you'll begin to notice when other voices are intruding or when you are using roundabout phrases. In time your sentences will gain rhythm and force. Reading aloud helps you to remember that, when you write, you are telling something to somebody. In fact another good technique is to visualize a particular person and pretend you are writing directly to that person.

Good writing is *honest*. Honest writing requires you to break through your fears of what other people might think of you and to tell what you know to be true.

Adding Details

Details give life to your ideas. As you write, you naturally concentrate on your ideas, but the reader will best remember a strong example or fact. Don't stuff in boring details, but instead catch the fact that proves your argument or the touch that brings a scene to life. Always remember: Give your reader the picture.

Adding Information

If a teacher asks for "more details," you probably have written a generalization with insufficient support. You need to slow down, take *one* idea at a time, and tell what it is based upon. You cannot assume that the reader agrees with you or knows what you're talking about. You have to say where you got your idea. This comes down to adding some of the following details to support your point:

- Examples

- Facts

- The logic behind your position

- Explanation of abstract words

Ideas are abstract and hard to picture. To be remembered, they must be embodied in concrete language—in pictures, in facts, in things that happened.

For example, here are three abstract statements:

> Gloria means what she says.
> The scene in the film was romantic.
> The paramecium displayed peculiar behavior.

Now here they are made more concrete:

> Gloria means what she says. She says she hates television, and she backs it up by refusing to date any man who watches TV.

> The soft focus of the camera and the violin music in the background heightened the romance of the scene.

Under the microscope, the paramecium displayed peculiar behavior. It doubled in size and turned purple.

Adding Sensory Details

The best writing appeals to our five senses. Your job as a writer is to put down words that will cause the reader to see, hear, smell, taste, or feel exactly what you experienced.

You can sharpen your senses with "here and now" exercises.

- Observe and write exactly what you see, feel, smell, taste, and hear moment by moment. Expand your descriptions until they become very specific.

- Write a paragraph describing a memory you have of a smell, a taste, a sight, a sound, a feeling (either a touch or a sensation).

- Describe one object completely—an orange, a frying pan, a leaf—using as many sensory details as possible.

These exercises will help build the habit of including careful observation in your writing.

Adding Word Power

Never underestimate the power of one good word. It's worth taking a look at each word in your sentence or paragraph to see if you can do better.

Choose words that are

- Concrete rather than abstract

- Short rather than long

- Simple rather than complex

- Informative rather than impressive

- Personal rather than impersonal

Don't just pull a word out of a thesaurus. Instead, choose words that are familiar to you and that say exactly what you mean.

REPETITION: BAD, NOT-SO-BAD, AND GOOD

Repetition can make your writing dull, but certain forms of repetition are necessary or even powerful.

■ BAD REPETITION

How to Avoid Repeating a Word

- Use a pronoun—*it, she, he,* or *they.* Repeating pronouns is usually not a problem. Make sure, however, that *it* clearly refers to a previous word and that the reader will know who *he* or *she* is. Avoid sentences like "His father told him that he would soon lose consciousness." (Who would lose consciousness?)

- Combine sentences. A simple *and* can save you from needless repetition and choppiness. See pages 177–78 for other ways to combine two short sentences.

- Go easy with the *Thesaurus.* Synonyms do not always have the same meanings, and even if they do, the tone may not be right. Replacing "cow" with "bovine" can lead to terrible writing. Generally don't use a word that is unfamiliar to you—you are likely to misuse it.

Avoid Repeating a Point or a Fact

Of course you will repeat your central idea—though not word for word—at key moments in your essay, especially in your conclusion. Nevertheless, making the same point in the same words over and over can seem dull-witted.

- Your conclusion should not repeat your introduction word for word. For alternatives, see page 84.

- If a fact is important, find the right place for it. Don't use the same example in two paragraphs.

- In an essay about a work of literature, do not repeat the title and the author's name in every paragraph.

▓ Not-So-Bad Repetition

Students often fret over repeating a word, but some repetition is natural and unobtrusive. In an essay about blogging, you will need to use the words *blog, blogger,* and *blogging,* and should not strain to find replacements.

▓ Good Repetition: Parallel Structure

Parallel structure—repeating certain words for clarity and emphasis—makes forceful sentences.

> To be honest is not necessarily to be brutal.

Famous quotations are often based on parallel structure.

> I came, I saw, I conquered.
>
> —Julius Caesar

> It was the best of times, it was the worst of times, it was the age of wisdom, it was the age of foolishness, it was the epoch of belief, it was the epoch of incredulity, it was the season of Light, it was the season of Darkness, it was the spring of hope, it was the winter of despair . . .
>
> —Charles Dickens

> Ask not what your country can do for you; ask what you can do for your country.
>
> —John F. Kennedy

For the correct usage of parallel structure, see page 58.

ELIMINATING INAPPROPRIATE LANGUAGE

Inappropriate language includes slang, vulgarity, and all expressions that demean or exclude people. To avoid offending your reader, examine both the words you use and their underlying assumptions.

Slang

Words you use commonly with your friends can distract many readers.

* Replace *kids* with *children, crap* with *garbage,* and *guy* with *man* or *boy.*

* Don't repeat *really* in every other sentence.

* Avoid IM abbreviations such as *u* for *you.*

Bigoted Word Choices

Some wording is prejudiced or impolite or outdated:

Eliminate name-calling, slurs, or derogatory nicknames. Instead, refer to groups by the names they use for themselves. For example, use *African Americans* (not *colored people*), *Asian* (not *Oriental*). If you criticize a group, explain your position rather than tossing in a nasty phrase.

Replace words using *man* or the *-ess* ending with nonsexist terms. For example, use *flight attendant* (not *stewardess*), *mechanic* (not *repairman*), *leader* or *diplomat* (not *statesman*).

False Assumptions

Some statements are based on hidden biases. Look hard at references to any group—even one you belong to.

Check for stereotyping about innate abilities or flaws in members of a group. For example, all women are not maternal, all lawyers are not devious, all Southerners are not racist, and all Japanese are not industrious. Many clichés are based in stereotypes: *absent-minded professor, dumb jock, Latin temper.*

Check assumptions that certain jobs are best filled by certain ethnic groups or one sex. For example, all nurses aren't women; all mechanics aren't men; all ballet dancers aren't Russian.

Watch for inconsistency. The following list assumes that everyone is a white man unless otherwise specified:

> two Republicans, a Democrat, an Independent, a woman, and an African American

Instead, use

> three Republicans, two Democrats, and an Independent

Faulty Pronoun Usage

Check pronouns for bias:

> Each Supreme Court justice should have *his clerk* attend the conference.

* One option for revision is to use *his or her.*

> Each Supreme Court justice should have *his or her* clerk attend the conference.

* A better solution is to use the plural throughout.

> The Supreme Court justices should have *their* clerks attend the conference.

* Often the most graceful solution is to eliminate the pronoun.

> Each Supreme Court justice should have a clerk attend the conference.

You can find more help with pronoun choice in "Consistent Pronouns" (pages 21–23).

Trimming Wordiness

Often we think that people are impressed by a writer who uses big words and long sentences. Actually, people are more impressed by a writer who is *clear.*

Cut Empty Words

Some words sound good but carry no clear meaning. Omitting them will often make the sentence sharper.

experience	the fact that
situation	really
is a man who	thing, something
personality	in life
in today's society	very
proceeded to	

In the following examples, the first version is wordy; the second version is trim.

> The fire was a terrifying situation and a depressing experience for all of us.
> The fire terrified and depressed all of us.

> Carmen is a woman who has a tempestuous personality.
> Carmen is tempestuous.

> The reason she quit was because of the fact that she was sick.
> She quit because of illness.

> Anger is something we all feel.
> We all feel anger.

In addition, *that* often can be cut.

> He said that he was sorry.
> He said he was sorry.

Avoid Redundancy—Pointless Repetition

> He married his wife twelve years ago.
> He married twelve years ago.

> She wore a scarf that was pink in color.
> She wore a pink scarf.

> Living a life of poverty is exhausting.
> Living in poverty is exhausting.

Be Direct

Tell what something *is* rather than what it *isn't*.

> Captain Bligh was not a very nice man.
> Captain Bligh was a tyrant.

Replace Weak Intensifiers: *Really, Very, Quite, Rather, Somewhat, Definitely*

These words don't add force but often dilute the impact of the word that follows.

> William was rather snobbish.
> William was a snob.

Replace Fancy or Technical Words

You can replace *utilize* with *use* and *coronary thrombosis* with *heart attack* and bring your paper down to earth. Some subjects may require technical language, but in general, strive to use everyday words. For example, *male* and *female* are appropriate for biology class, but use *man* and *woman* for general purposes.

When you trim, don't worry that your papers will be too short. For length add examples and further thoughts. Look at the topic from a different viewpoint. Add points, not just words.

Using Strong Verbs

One of the quickest ways to add excitement and forcefulness to your writing is to replace limp verbs with strong ones. Three simple guidelines can help you to do so:

- Replace passive verbs with active verbs.

- Get rid of *being* verbs.

- Choose dynamic verbs.

Replace Passive Verbs with Active Verbs

You can write a verb in *active voice* or *passive voice:*

Passive:	An inspiring talk was given by the president of the college.
Active:	The president of the college gave an inspiring talk.
Passive:	Several safety precautions should be taken before attempting rock climbing.
Active:	Rock climbers should take several safety precautions.

More often than not, you can put energy into your writing by converting passive verbs into active ones.

People often use passive verbs when they do not want to name the person who did the action. The passive construction is less direct and therefore less revealing:

A pedestrian was struck down at the intersection.

The position of marketing director has been eliminated as of July 1.

Mistakes were made.

Get Rid of *Being* Verbs

Being verbs, like *is* and *are,* sap the energy from your writing. The verb *to be* comes in eight forms:

am, is, are, was, were, be, being, been

Often you can replace *being* verbs with forceful verbs. Go through your writing, circle every form of *be,* and then do your best to replace each one with a dynamic verb—a verb that communicates specific action or creates a picture.

> The audience was irate. People were jumping out of their seats and were coming into the aisles.

This example has three *being* forms. Eliminating the three *being* verbs makes the sentence tighter and more dynamic:

> The irate audience jumped out of their seats and flooded the aisles.

Watch out especially for *there is, there are, there was, there were, it is, it was.* You can usually eliminate these empty constructions:

> It is depressing to watch the national news.

> Watching the national news depresses me.

> There are three people who influenced my choice of career.

> Three people influenced my choice of career.

Save *being* verbs for when you mean a state of being:

> I am totally exhausted.

> She was born on Bastille Day.

Choose Dynamic Verbs

Verbs, because they show action, are usually the strongest words in a sentence, the words that give life to your writing. Keep an eye out for verbs that make a picture:

> Smiling his painted smile, the governor circled through the crowd.

> To arrest their attention, I hobbled across the yard and flung myself on the ground.

> Hedy Lamarr lounged her way through life.

> The whole team came roaring down on the umpire when he stumbled over second base and tripped the base runner.

Varying Your Sentences

The same idea can be put in many different ways, and every sentence has movable parts. To get more music or drama into your style, try reading your writing aloud. When you come across choppy or monotonous sentences, use some of the following techniques.

Write an Important Sentence Several Ways

You can turn a sentence that troubles you into a sentence that pleases you. Instead of fiddling with a word here and a word there, try writing five completely different sentences—each with the same idea. One could be long, one short, one a generalization, one a picture, and so forth. Often you'll find that your first isn't your best. If you play with several possibilities, you'll come up with the one you want. This technique works especially well for improving introductions and conclusions.

Use Short Sentences Frequently

Short sentences are the meat and bones of good writing.

- They can simplify an idea.
- They can dramatize a point.
- They can create suspense.
- They can add rhythm.
- They can be blunt and forceful.

If you're getting tangled in too many words, a few short sentences will often get you through.

Remember, however, that you must use a period even between very short but complete sentences:

> It was a rainy Monday. I was sitting at my desk. I heard a knock at the door. The doorknob turned. The barrel of a shotgun inched through the doorway.

Lengthen Choppy Sentences

Using *only* short sentences can make your writing monotonous. If you want to lengthen a sentence, the simplest way is to add concrete information.

> The book was boring.

> The author's long descriptions of rooms in which nothing and no one ever moved made the book boring.

Combine Choppy Sentences

Combine two short sentences back to back. Here are three ways:

- Put a semicolon between them.

  > Kitty expected Anna Karenina to wear a lavender dress to the ball; Anna chose black.

  (Be sure each half is a complete sentence.)

- Put a comma followed by one of these connectors:

but	and	for
or	so	yet
nor		

  > Kitty expected Anna Karenina to wear a lavender dress to the ball, but Anna chose black.

- Put a semicolon followed by a transition word and a comma. Here are the most common transition words.

however	for example	meanwhile
therefore	furthermore	nevertheless
instead	in other words	on the other hand
besides		

  > Kitty expected Anna Karenina to wear a lavender dress to the ball; instead, Anna chose black.

Combine sentences to highlight the major point. Often sentences contain two or more facts. You can show the relationship between these facts so that the most important one stands out.

> Although Kitty expected Anna Karenina to wear a lavender dress to the ball, Anna chose black.

In the following examples, the first of each set gives two ideas equal weight. The revised sentence emphasizes one idea.

> Martha Grimes was a college professor. She became a best-selling mystery writer.
> Before she became a best-selling mystery writer, Martha Grimes was a college professor.

> I love Earl. He barks at the slightest sound.
> I love Earl even though he barks at the slightest sound.

> Brad lost a contact lens. He had one blue eye and one brown eye.
> Because Brad lost a contact lens, he had one blue eye and one brown eye.

Notice that the halves of the revised sentences can be reversed.

> Although Earl barks at the slightest sound, I still love him.

Usually the sentence gains strength when the most interesting point comes last.

Insert the gist of one sentence inside another.

> Sheila Baldwin makes a fine living as a photographer. She has a great eye for unusual pictures. She is very adventuresome.

> Sheila Baldwin, with her great eye for unusual pictures and her spirit of adventure, makes a fine living as a photographer.

The problem with most choppy sentences is that one after another starts with the subject of the sentence—in this case, *Sheila* or *she*. Sometimes you can use *who* (for people) or *which* (for things) to start an insertion. Sometimes you can reduce the insertion to a word or two.

> I interviewed Nell Partin, who is the mayor, about the sanitation strike.

> I interviewed Nell Partin, the mayor, about the sanitation strike.

Vary the Beginnings of Your Sentences

It's easy to fall into starting every sentence the same way. Here are some alternatives to the usual noun-verb or pronoun-verb pattern.

- Use a transition word like *however, moreover, instead.* See the list on page 80.

- Start with an adverb that describes the action.

  Warily, he opened the door.

- Start with an *-ing* phrase before the main sentence.

  Responding to critics, the president held a news conference.

- Combine two sentences.

Give Your Sentences a Strong Ending

The beginning is worth sixty cents, what's in the middle is worth forty cents, but the end is worth a dollar.

  I walked into the room, looked around at all the flowers my friends had sent, took a deep breath, and collapsed onto the sofa in tears.

  When the nights grow cool and foggy and the full moon rises after the day's harvest, Madeline, so the story goes, roams the hills in search of revenge.

  What Louie Gallagher received, after all the plea-bargaining and haggling and postponements and hearings, was a ten-year sentence.

To stress the most important parts of your sentence, tuck in interrupters or insertions. Put transitions or minor information into the middle of your sentence.

  He argues, as you probably know, even with statues.

  From my point of view, however, that's a mistake.

  The interior decoration, designed by his cousin, looked gaudy.

Remember to put commas on *both* sides of the insertion.

Imitate Good Writers

Take a close look at the writings of some of your favorite authors. A good exercise is to pick out a sentence or a paragraph that you particularly like. Read it aloud once or twice; then copy it over several times to get the feel of the language. Now study it closely and try to write an imitation of it. Use the sentence or paragraph as a model, but think up your own ideas and words. This exercise can rapidly expand your power to vary your sentences.

RECOGNIZING CLICHÉS

A cliché is a *predictable* word, phrase, or statement. If it sounds very familiar, if it comes very easily, it's probably a cliché. Clichés are comfortable, and they are usually true. In conversation clichés are often acceptable, but in writing they can either annoy or bore the reader. Learn to recognize clichés and replace them with fresher, sharper language.

Recognize Clichés

Some clichés are old sayings; others are expressions that are either worn out or trendy.

Nobody's perfect	Happy camper
Slept like a log	Head over heels
Smooth as silk	Mother Nature
By leaps and bounds	Easier said than done
Spread like wildfire	User-friendly
Don't judge a book by its cover	Cool
That special someone	

This year's new expression is next year's cliché. (Try saying "groovy" to your friends.)

Eliminate Clichés

- Often you can simply omit a cliché—you don't need it. The essay is better without it.

- At other times replace the cliché by saying what you mean. Give the details.

- Look out for clichés in your conclusion; that's where they love to gather.

- Make up your own comparisons and descriptions. Have fun being creative.

KEEPING A JOURNAL

Keeping a journal is one of the best ways to grow as a writer. Writing just for yourself helps you put your thoughts and feelings into words, overcome writer's block, and develop your own personal style. You will also discover truths you didn't know—about yourself and about many topics. Some of your journal writing can later be developed into complete essays or stories.

A journal is different from a diary (a day-by-day list of what you do). A journal can include memories, feelings, observations, hopes. It gives you the opportunity to try your hand at different types of writing, so aim for variety in your entries.

Some Guidelines for Keeping a Journal

- Write several times a week for at least ten minutes.

- Write in ink or create a folder on your computer. Date each entry.

- If you have no topic, write whatever comes into your head or choose one of the suggestions from the list given here.

- While you write, don't worry about correctness. Write as spontaneously and as honestly as you can, and let your thoughts and words flow freely.

- At your leisure reread your entries and make any corrections or additions you like. If you use your computer, print or back up your journal. Remember, this journal is for *you*, and it will be a source of delight to you in years to come.

Some Suggestions for Journal Entries

Blow off steam.

Tell your favorite story about yourself when you were little.

Disagree with someone else's opinion, based upon your personal experience.

Respond to a movie, a TV program, a book, an article, a concert, a song.

Write a letter to someone and say what you can't say face to face.

Describe in full detail a place you know and love—or a place you visited often as a child.

Remember on paper your very first boyfriend or girlfriend.

Relate, using present tense, a memorable dream you've had.

Tell how your view of an aunt or uncle has changed.

Analyze the personal trait that gets you in trouble most often.

Relate an incident in which you were proud (or ashamed) of yourself.

Describe your dream house.

Capture on paper some object—such as a toy or article of clothing—that you loved as a child or love now.

Tell about someone you know who was considered "odd."

Write down a family story. Include when and where you have heard it.

Set down a "here and now" scene: record sensory details right at the moment you're experiencing them.

Go to a public place and observe people. Write down your observations.

Explain your most pressing problem at present.

Trace the history of your hair.

Take one item from today's newspaper and give your thoughts about it.

Choose something you'd like to know more about—or need to know more about—and tell why.

Commit yourself in writing to doing something you've always wanted to do but never have.

Write about yourself as a writer.

Analyze your relationship to food, to medication, to budgeting, or to time.

POSTSCRIPT

You do your best work when you take pleasure in a job. You write best when you know something about the topic and know what you want to stress. So, when you can, write about a topic you've lived with and have considered over time. When you *have* to write about a topic that seems boring or difficult, get to know it for a while, until it makes sense to you. Start with what is clear to you and you will write well.

Don't quit too soon. Sometimes a few more changes, a little extra attention to fine points, or a new paragraph written on a separate piece of paper will transform an acceptable essay into an essay that really pleases you. Through the time you spend writing and rewriting, you will discover what is most important to say.

■ AN INVITATION

Rules of Thumb was written for you, so we welcome your comments about it and about *Good Measures: A Practice Book to Accompany Rules of Thumb*. Please write directly to us:

Jay Silverman and Diana Roberts Wienbroer
Department of English
Nassau Community College
Garden City, New York 11530-6793

If you would like to purchase individual copies of *Rules of Thumb* directly from McGraw-Hill, please go to:

www.mhprofessional.com

For textbook orders and examination copies, you can also call:

1-800-338-3987

Visit McGraw-Hill's Higher Education website at
<www.mhhe.com>.

A LIST OF VALUABLE SOURCES

The sources given here may be listed in a menu of choices on your library's home page. If you do not find an electronic version, ask the librarian for the print or film version.

You may be able to access some of these sources directly on the Web; when you find an article on the Web that is available only to subscribers, check to see if your library has free access.

INDEXES AND DATABASES

ABI/INFORM Research

Academic Onefile

Academic Search Premier

American National Biography

AP Photo Archive

Business Source Premier

Custom Newspapers

ERIC
(educational resources)

General Science Collection

Health & Wellness Resource Center

History Resource Center

Humanities Index

InfoTrac

LexisNexis

Literature Resource Center

MagillOnLiterature Plus

Medline

MLA (Modern Language Association) International Bibliography

NetLibrary

New York Times

Newspaper Source

Opposing Viewpoints Resource Center

ProQuest Selectable Full Text Newspapers

PsycInfo

Readers' Guide Full Text

ScienceDirect

SocINDEX

Westlaw

REFERENCE PAGES

Internet Public Library	http://www.ipl.org/
Librarians' Index to the Internet	http://lii.org/
RefDesk (Virtual Reference Desk)	http://www.refdesk.com/
Voice of the Shuttle (general humanities resources)	http://vos.ucsb.edu/

ELECTRONIC TEXTS

Alex: Catalogue of Electronic Texts	http://infomotions.com/alex/
Bartleby: Great Books Online	http://www.bartleby.com/
The Bible Online	http://www.biblegateway.com/
The Complete Works of William Shakespeare	http://the-tech.mit.edu/ Shakespeare/works.html
Digital Book Index	http://www.digitalbookindex.org/ about.htm

E-Server at Iowa State University	http://eserver.org/
Gutenberg	http://www.gutenberg.net/
Page by Page Books	http://pagebypagebooks.com

NEWS SOURCES ONLINE

Note that most news organizations maintain a website with at least some material from their current issues or programs. Sources listed here allow free searches through their archives, although there may be a fee for the article itself.

Chronicle of Higher Education http://www.ALdaily.com/
Arts and Letters Daily
(with updated reviews and links to news sources)

National Public Radio	http://www.npr.org/
Newslink (links to magazines and newspapers)	http://newslink.org/
New York Times	http://www.nytimes.com/
Public Broadcasting *System*	http://www.pbs.org/

STATISTICAL SOURCES

American Statistical Index	http://www.fedstats.gov/
Bureau of Census Reports	http://www.census.gov/
FedWorld	http://www.fedworld.gov/
Statistical Resources *on the Web*	http://www.lib.umich.edu/ govdocs/statsnew
World Fact Book	http://www.bartleby.com/151

See also individual federal agencies' websites.

HELP WITH STYLE, GRAMMAR, AND USAGE

Merriam-Webster, eds. *Merriam Webster's Collegiate Dictionary.*
    11th ed. Springfield, MA: Merriam-Webster, 2003. Print.
    Also at http://www.merriam-webster.com

Burchfield, R. W., ed. *The New Fowler's Modern English Usage.* 3rd ed. New York: Oxford, 2000. Print. A thorough coverage on word usage.

Jack Lynch's Page:
Guide to Grammar and   http://andromeda.rutgers.edu/
Style   ~jlynch/Writing

Ammer, Christine. *American Heritage Dictionary of Idioms.* Boston: Houghton, 1997. Print. An explanation of the meaning of phrases and when to use which preposition in a phrase (especially helpful for ESL).

Foreign Word: Online   http://www.foreignword.com/
Dictionaries and Free
Translation Tools

The Free Dictionary: Idioms   http://idioms.thefreedictionary.com/

HELP WITH FORMAT FOR RESEARCH PAPERS

American Psychological Association. *Publication Manual of the American Psychological Association.* 6th ed. Washington, DC: American Psychological Association, 2010. Print. Also see their website http://www.apastyle.org/

Modern Language Association of America. *MLA Handbook for Writers of Research Papers.* 7th ed. New York: MLA, 2009. Print.

RESOURCES FOR EVALUATING INFORMATION

Evaluating Websites: http://www.library.cornell.edu/
Criteria and Tools   olinuris/ref/research/webeval.html

FAIR (Fairness and   http://www.fair.org/
Accuracy in Reporting)

Fact Check (Annenberg   http://www.factcheck.org/
School of Journalism at
Univ. of Penn)

Urban Legends   http://www.snopes.com/

ABOUT THE AUTHORS

A graduate of Amherst College and the University of Virginia, **Jay Silverman** has received Fulbright, Mellon, and NEH fellowships. Dr. Silverman has taught at Virginia Highlands Community College and at Nassau Community College where he received the Honors Program award for Excellence in Teaching and where he also teaches in the College Bound Program of the Nassau County Mental Health Association and in NCC's Achilles Program for gifted students with disabilities. Since the death of his wife, Beverly Jensen, Dr. Silverman has edited her fiction; Stephen King included "Wake" in *2007 Best American Short Stories*, and Viking Press will publish her novel *The Sisters from Hardscrabble Bay* in 2010.

Elaine Hughes taught writing for more than twenty-five years, primarily at Hinds Community College in Raymond, Mississippi, and at Nassau Community College. She also conducted many writing workshops for the Esalen Institute and other organizations. In 2000 she won a Mississippi Arts Council grant for creative nonfiction. She is the author of *Writing from the Inner Self*. In 2001 Elaine Hughes passed away after more than twenty years of victories over breast cancer.

As Chair of the English Department of Nassau Community College, **Diana Roberts Wienbroer** coordinated a department of 150 faculty members and served on the Executive Council of the Association of Departments of English. Besides teaching writing for over forty years, both in Texas and New York, she has studied and taught film criticism. Since her retirement from NCC, she has taught seminars on Internet research and effective business writing.

The authors have also written *Rules of Thumb for Business Writers*, available from McGraw-Hill.

INDEX

TROUBLESHOOTING GUIDE

PROBLEMS WITH CORRECTNESS AND STYLE

Punctuation
Start with pp. 31–37 (comma vs. period, run-on sentences, comma splices, sentence fragments).
See pp. 38–39 for comma rules.
See pp. 40–43 for semicolons, colons, dashes, and parentheses.

Apostrophes, see p. 20.

Quotation marks, see pp. 44–47. Also see pp. 82–83.

Titles, see p. 48.

Spelling
Start with pp. 3–10 (the most commonly confused words).
For the basic spelling rules, see pp. 13–15.
For common misspellings, study the examples on pp. 13–15.

Pronoun errors
Singulars and plurals, see pp. 21–23.
I vs. *me*, see pp. 24–25.

Verb errors
Agreement of subject and verb, see pp. 54–55.
Passive verbs, see pp. 174–75.
Verb tenses, see pp. 49–55.

Word endings
Start with pp. 56–57.
Also study pp. 13, 20, 51, and 54–55.

Parallel structure, see pp. 58 and 169.

Dangling constructions, see p. 59.

Awkward writing, wordiness, and repetition
Start with pp. 165 and 172–73.
Study pp. 168–69 (repetition)
Study pp. 26–27 and 58–60.

Sentence variety, see pp. 176–80.